· T R O P H I E S ·

English-Language Learners
TEACHER'S GUIDE
Grade 5

Harcourt

Orlando   Boston   Dallas   Chicago   San Diego

Visit *The Learning Site!*
www.harcourtschool.com

Copyright © by Harcourt, Inc.

All rights reserved. No part of this publication may be reproduced or transmitted in any form or by any means, electronic or mechanical, including photocopy, recording, or any information storage and retrieval system, without permission in writing from the publisher.

Permission is hereby granted to individual teachers using the corresponding student's textbook or kit as the major vehicle for regular classroom instruction to photocopy Copying Masters from this publication in classroom quantities for instructional use and not for resale. Requests for information on other matters regarding duplication of this work should be addressed to School Permissions and Copyrights, Harcourt, Inc., 6277 Sea Harbor Drive, Orlando, Florida 32887-6777. Fax: 407-345-2418.

HARCOURT and the Harcourt Logo are trademarks of Harcourt, Inc., registered in the United States of America and/or other jurisdictions.

Printed in the United States of America

ISBN 0-15-329338-1

1 2 3 4 5 6 7 8 9 10 082 10 09 08 07 06 05 04 03 02 01

Table of Contents

© Harcourt

© Harcourt

English-Language Learners Resource Kit Teacher's Guide

TROPHIES *English-Language Learners Kit* is designed to provide teachers with the materials for 30–45 minutes of daily instruction to be used in addition and connected to the basic instruction in the mainstream English classroom. Materials are designed to help English-language learners (ELLs) read, write, comprehend, and speak at personally and academically proficient levels. These skills, coupled with the instruction in TROPHIES, will enable ELLs to become proficient in English.

The Kit includes the following components:

Grade Level	Components
Kindergarten	*Alphabet Books Collection, Teacher's Resource Book, English-Language Learners Big Book*
I	*English-Language Learners Books Collection, Teacher's Guide,* laminated lap boards
2–6	*English-Language Learners Books Collection, Teacher's Guide,* laminated lap boards

How to Use This Guide

Each 6-page lesson is tied directly to the corresponding lesson in TROPHIES. The *English-Language Learners Teacher's Guide* lessons provide opportunities to preteach and reteach the skills students must master. Pages vi–xxi provide additional information for utilizing the 30–45-minute period.

Following is a brief description of what appears on each lesson page. Pages are linked to specific sections of TROPHIES lessons cited in the **BEFORE** and **AFTER** boxes.

■ **Page I**   BEFORE/AFTER   **Building Background and Vocabulary**

The teacher **accesses students' prior knowledge by building broad background concept(s)** important to both the TROPHIES selection and the *English-Language Learners Book*. This provides a foundation for the specific background building done for the TROPHIES selection (page 2) and for the *English-Language Learners Book* (page 3). The teacher **preteaches and reteaches selection vocabulary** using the TROPHIES Reteach Vocabulary Teaching Transparency and context sentences. The **Fluency Practice** feature suggests ways that students can demonstrate their reading and speaking fluency daily.

© Harcourt

■ **Page 2**   BEFORE/AFTER   **Reading the TROPHIES selection**

After **building specific background for the TROPHIES selection**, the teacher **preteaches the focus skill**. Students are encouraged to use graphic organizers to apply to the selection what they have learned about the skill. The teacher uses the **directed reading** section to guide students through the TROPHIES selection. Scaffolded questions are used to monitor comprehension. The focus skill will be **retaught** after both the TROPHIES selection and the *English-Language Learners Book* have been read.

■ **Page 3**   BEFORE/AFTER   **Reading the *English-Language Learners Book***

After **building specific background for the *English-Language Learners Book***, the teacher introduces the concept words, 5–8 high-utility words from the *English-Language Learners Book*. The teacher uses the **directed reading** section to guide students through the *English-Language Learners Book*. The teacher **reteaches the focus skill** and asks students to apply it through the *English-Language Learners Book*.

■ **Pages 4–5**   BEFORE/AFTER   **Writing and Grammar**

The **writing lessons** in this *Teacher's Guide* parallel those in TROPHIES, but are scaffolded, beginning with shared writing and progressing to interactive writing and independent writing. The rate at which students move from one type of writing to the next varies with grade level. Student-generated writing is used for fluency practice and as working models for revising practice. The **grammar instruction** parallels that in TROPHIES. An initial emphasis on oral grammar helps students develop an ear for the English language. Students then apply knowledge of the grammar skill to their writing, noting how and when it was used and correcting errors.

■ **Page 6**   **Copying Master**

The activities on this reproducible page provide practice with various parts of the lesson. Notes to the teacher give suggestions and tips for use.

© Harcourt

English-Language Development Fluency Stages

ELLs in any given classroom may span a range of fluency stages. In terms of comprehension, it is not necessary for every student to understand every word the teacher says. Considerable language acquisition will occur with even a modest percentage of comprehensible input. The following criteria are given for five identified stages of fluency. Students at each stage can be expected to continue behaviors from the previous stage.

1. Beginning English-Language Learners

Listening/Speaking

- respond non verbally or with one or two words and short phrases
- ask simple questions
- participate in songs, chants, and rhymes
- use present-tense verbs and simple plurals correctly
- participate in group-generated stories

Reading

- decode but have difficulty with English phonemic awareness
- comprehend simple content
- begin to read single words and short phrases

Writing

- copy, label, and list
- write familiar words and phrases

The teacher should

- model, rephrase, and repeat sentence patterns and vocabulary
- use the Total Physical Response (TPR) method in which the teacher gives a command involving an overt physical response to which students respond. Initially, the teacher performs the action with students, but eventually the students perform it on their own.

2. Early Intermediate English-Language Learners

Listening/Speaking

- begin to model verb tenses, such as present participles
- ask and answer simple questions about familiar content
- participate in face-to-face conversations with peers
- begin to self-check and self-correct

Reading

- comprehend and recall main ideas of a simple story or other content
- improve pronunciation and phonemic awareness
- read student-generated text

Writing

- use graphic organizers and writing frames
- write simple questions and answers

The teacher should

- provide opportunities for students to negotiate for meaning (See page xiv.)
- use pictures, graphic organizers, and sentence frames
- use interactive writing

© Harcourt

3. Intermediate English-Language Learners

Listening/Speaking

- express creative thoughts and use original language
- use complete simple sentences
- produce sustained conversation on a variety of topics

Reading

- interact with a variety of print

Writing

- transfer reading and oral language to writing
- write for a variety of purposes
- participate fully in editing

The teacher should

- provide shared, paired, and independent reading opportunities
- model and provide practice for using expanded verb tenses

4. Early Advanced English-Language Learners

Listening/Speaking

- generally comprehend all usual English speech
- demonstrate adequate pronunciation and grammar usage

Reading

- use a variety of reading strategies
- use various study skills

Writing

- use extended written production in all content areas
- use adjectives, adverbs, and figurative language in writing

The teacher should

- teach, model, and allow for expanded discourse in writing and reading

5. Advanced English-Language Learners

Listening/Speaking

- comprehend concrete and abstract topics and concepts
- use effortless, fluent speech

Reading

- read grade-level materials with limited difficulty

Writing

- write to meet social needs and academic demands

The teacher should

- teach, model, and allow for practice of complex sentence structures

© Harcourt

Learning to Read and Reading to Learn
Distinguishing Between ELD and SDAIE Instruction

Like students everywhere, ELLs move from learning to read to reading to learn. Tailoring instruction for students who are new to English involves moving from English Language Development (ELD) to Specially Designed Academic Instruction in English (SDAIE). The differences are as follows:

English Language Development (formerly known as ESL) refers to the beginning stages of fluency. It is characterized by beginning literacy and language development, not grade-level content. Though ELD is important for ELLs at all stages of language acquisition, it is crucial for those students in the Beginning and Early Intermediate stages.

The components of an **ELD** lesson are as follows:

Access Prior Knowledge

- Use primary language as necessary.

Provide Comprehensible Input

- Introduce vocabulary, concepts, and language patterns, using rich context.
- Speak slowly and clearly.
- Avoid idioms.
- Use cognates whenever possible.
- Chunk instruction for ten minutes, followed by two minutes of peer interaction in students' primary language as necessary.
- Use gestures, facial expressions, and dramatization.
- Use visuals such as realia, pictures, graphic organizers, and videos.

Check for Understanding

- Elicit responses in ways that do not require oral production.
- Paraphrase, repeat, and expand on what was taught before asking students for confirmation of understanding.
- Allow for extensive student-to-student interaction in students' primary language as necessary.
- Provide many opportunities for practice of new language patterns, concepts, and vocabulary.

Foster Beginning Literacy

- Link instruction to students' background knowledge.
- Make purposes clear.
- Scaffold activities by teacher modeling, cooperative group practice, and individual use.

Assessment

- Focus on language development.

© Harcourt

The components of a **SDAIE** lesson are as follows:

Tap Prior Knowledge

- Access knowledge of content, vocabulary, and sentence structures.

Contextualize the Lesson

- Scaffold the instruction.
- Reuse vocabulary and key concepts in a variety of ways.
- Summarize the instruction after each lesson.

Modify the Text

- Develop background knowledge to initiate the lesson.
- Preview in primary language.
- Use read-alouds followed by group discussions.
- Provide a variety of high-interest, low-readability texts.
- Model reading and writing by thinking aloud strategies as you use them.
- Have students develop their own dictionaries. (See page xi.)
- Provide a variety of opportunities for student-generated writing.
- Use student-generated text for a variety of purposes, such as writing practice, grammar practice, and reading fluency.

Allow for Student-to-Student Negotiation for Meaning

- Have students work in cooperative groups.
- Encourage higher levels of student discourse, including stating point of view, giving opinions, and paraphrasing.

Teach Study Skills

- Provide graphic organizers and focused questions to help students set a purpose.
- Have students practice completing graphic organizers as they read or listen.
- Give instruction on multiple-meaning words.
- Use reference materials.

Assessment

- Check students' facial expressions and body language frequently for evidence of understanding.
- Have students demonstrate understanding by asking them to frequently paraphrase what they've just learned.

© Harcourt

Making and Using Picture File Cards

A picture card file is a valuable instructional tool, particularly when students provide input and create the file.

First, gather magazines, catalogs, calendars, and the like. Then direct students to find pictures that are connected in some way to the content you will be studying. Students must provide some rationale to the class or small group for their choices. If the group agrees on a picture, the student who selected it glues it onto an index card. This process can generate as many as 100 cards in less than one hour. In addition to saving valuable teacher time, students are engaged in many higher-level thinking skills such as classifying, categorizing, evaluating, justifying, analyzing, making judgments, listening, and speaking. Following are a few of the ways you can use your picture card file:

■ provide comprehensible input during background building and direct instruction
■ stimulate discussion including questions, descriptions, and story-telling
■ stimulate ideas for writing

Making and Using Big Books

It can be difficult to find a Big Book that emphasizes exactly the content, language patterning, and vocabulary for specific needs. By making your own Big Books, you can embed specific concepts and vocabulary with the right patterning in a comprehensible way to, for example, access prior knowledge and build background.

First, select and research a topic. Identify key concepts and vocabulary you want to cover. Then write some phrases to form the language pattern.

The following pattern models expository text—topic sentence/supporting details/closing sentence:

> **Key pattern phrase**
> **First key concept**
> **Second key concept**
> **Third key concept**
> **Closing pattern phrase**

Big Book illustrations run the gamut from a collage of magazine clippings to geometric patterns to hand-drawn artwork. First, read the text straight through without stopping for definitions or explanations. Students should feel the rhythm of the language patterns. After the first reading, ask students for their responses, and encourage questions. Then conduct a second reading with the emphasis on meaning. Encourage discussion. You may want to read a third time with students, asking them to read parts of the text, or as much as they can handle.

© Harcourt

The Language-Functional Classroom: Using "Living Walls"

In a language-functional environment, every piece of text presented in class is posted on the walls to be read and reread, processed, discussed, and augmented daily. The walls are said to be alive because they grow in direct proportion with students' own language growth.

At the start of every thematic unit, perhaps six times per school year, the walls are blank. A thematic idea provides the seed that is germinated by its connection to students' backgrounds and prior knowledge. The walls become the home for completed graphic organizers, sentence patterning charts, and lists of words provided by and with students as they acquire the content of the subject at hand. The walls may also include student artwork and other pictorial representations of vocabulary and concepts. To fully utilize living walls, students must contribute to their growth and use them daily.

A living wall might begin with a large sketch of the setting of the next reading selection. During a discussion of concepts and content vocabulary, the teacher would add both pictures and words to the sketch. Throughout the theme or unit of instruction, students and the teacher add to the walls together.

Language Dictionary and Language Journal

ELLs will feel ownership of their vocabulary acquisition if they are able to capture words and phrases in a **Language Dictionary**. This is a notebook or stapled set of pages in which students record new vocabulary. Periodically they may reorganize their Language Dictionaries alphabetically by recasting pages or sections of pages.

Selection vocabulary and concept vocabulary are prime candidates for inclusion in a student's Language Dictionary. Familiarity with selection vocabulary will enable ELLs to participate in vocabulary activities in the mainstream classroom and to have more success with the core selection and attendant ancillary pages. Familiarity with concept vocabulary provides ELLs with high-utility words and phrases to use both in speaking and in writing.

Students may enter a vocabulary word in their Language Dictionaries followed by a picture, definition in their first language, or English definition. As they recast their Language Dictionary pages, they may want to amplify their definitions, adding definitions or changing drawings and first-language definitions to definitions written in English.

Language Dictionaries should be a useful tool for students' writing assignments.

Similarly, a **Language Journal** is a simple notebook in which a student can record anything from ideas for writing assignments to daily journal entries. It may provide a means for the teacher to conduct informal assessments of student progress throughout the school year. Students may use it as a tool for reviewing what they've learned and as a resource for completing various assignments.

© Harcourt

Interactive Writing

Interactive writing is an excellent means of having students generate text under a teacher's supervision. This form of writing is most often used in kindergarten and first grade; however, beginning ELLs will benefit from this process:

1. Have students sit in a circle holding their lap boards. They should have an unobstructed view of the chart-paper stand or the board you are using.
2. Brainstorm a writing topic with students, ask them whether they have a question for observation about a content area, or provide a writing prompt.
3. Work with students to analyze the prompt and prewrite. Make sure students understand the writing objective. Write what students dictate to you.
4. Have students share with you the act of writing and the ideas of what to write. Allow students to come to the chart and write words and sentences. Prompt them with grammar and spelling tips as a review, and model grammar and spelling rules they have not yet learned. Use this student writing as a way to model correct letter formation, space between letters and words, spelling, punctuation, grammar, and writer's craft skills.
5. As you model correct grammar, spelling, and the like, have students practice writing the words and phrases correctly on their lap boards.
6. Think aloud about the structure and meaning of the text you are composing. Use explicit prompts to help students use the spelling and grammar they have learned.
7. Reread frequently with students during the composing of the text to monitor the message and to plan what to write next.
8. You may want to have students make a copy of the finished piece of writing either in their Language Journals or for publishing purposes.

Student-generated texts and frames are excellent reading and writing tools. Group Frames and Cooperative Strip Paragraphs are two techniques particularly useful in expository writing.

Group Frames This strategy is used to teach and model different writing forms. It can be used with students at most stages of language acquisition.

■ Provide a topic sentence based on the writing form to be used.

■ Students help plan the writing by brainstorming ideas, using graphic organizers, sketching their ideas, listing their ideas, and having substantive discussions.

■ Gather ideas from as many students as possible to give even the most reluctant students some ownership of the final product.

© Harcourt

Cooperative Strip Paragraphs This strategy is used to teach and model the writing process.

- Provide the topic sentence.

- Have students provide the supporting details from the graphic organizers or other brainstorming tools they developed.

- Students discuss what they will write and then write the sentences they have agreed upon. This strategy allows for a lot of negotiating for meaning and an anxiety-free environment for practice in developing any kind of text.

- Students revise and edit their own text.

- With modeling and practice, students will be able to generate their own topic sentences and supporting details.

Student-Generated Text This type of writing can and should be used for reading fluency practice.

- Students take a piece of text they have written and reread it together, highlighting what they find interesting or compelling.

- Students then read to see whether the writing makes sense and suggest revisions. For students at earlier stages of fluency, the teacher should suggest revisions based on ordering ideas, word substitution or sentence combining, adding, deleting, and so on.

- Model each change and discuss with students the reason for it. Then have students apply the changes to their work.

- Students should demonstrate their understanding of the benefits of the revision, noting in particular that the audience for whom the writing is intended will more readily understand the writer's message. They should also understand the revision process of reading and thinking about one's writing, rather than just physically writing, and the aggregate benefit of incorporating the suggestions of others.

- As students become increasingly comfortable with the revision process, teacher modeling should decrease as students move into more independent writing.

- After the revision, teach and model the editing process. As in the revision, students reread the writing and make suggestions to improve it in terms of spelling, punctuation, and so on. Students should never be expected to edit for a skill they have not yet been taught.

- Cooperative strip paragraphs can be used as authentic opportunities for modeling editing because there is less resistance to changing something of which no student has complete ownership.

- You may wish to create a final published copy of the text and distribute it for reading fluency practice either in a small group, with a partner, or silently.

© Harcourt

Strategies for Effective Language Acquisition

Negotiating for Meaning

ELLs maximize comprehensible input when they **negotiate for meaning**. These student-to-student discussions at any point in the lesson provide opportunities to practice new vocabulary, including academic language, and help students achieve an understanding of concepts and language forms. This provides a risk-free environment for problem-solving and fosters positive interdependence. ELLs will have opportunities to internalize meaning, not just memorize vocabulary and facts.

An effective way to promote the strategy of negotiating for meaning is to allow at least two minutes of student processing (oral or written) after every ten minutes of instruction. Students may sit in first-language groups during the instruction. After a 10-minute chunk, students should briefly turn to their neighbors for discussion. This way, they can process new concepts in their primary language before doing so in English.

The prompts at the right can be used by teachers initially and then by students as they work with a partner or in a small group to negotiate for meaning.

Predicting

With a title like this, what do you think the story will be about? What will happen next? Why do you think so? Turn to your partner and talk to each other about what might happen next.

Monitoring and Adjusting

After reading, what do you still want to know? What do you still not understand? Turn to your neighbor and ask a question that you still have about the story. Find the part that you still don't understand. What can you do to understand it?

Paraphrasing and Summarizing

Explain to a partner what you have just read. List the main points. What was the most interesting thing you read about? What did you learn?

© Harcourt

Assessment

Assessment should be authentic and performance-based. Teachers can use observation and informal chats with students to determine where they are and how much progress they have made.

As students work individually, in pairs, or in small groups, it is important to balance both promoting independence and providing support. This rubric and the accompanying Group Summary Record Form on page xvi can be used to record students' progress in oral fluency. You may want to tailor these tools to the needs of your students.

Oral Language Observation Rubric

	Beginning	Early Intermediate	Intermediate	Early Advanced	Advanced
Listening Comprehension	Does not understand simple conversation	Understands simple conversation with great difficulty	Understands most simple conversation spoken slowly with repetition	Understands nearly all simple conversation at normal speed with some repetition	Understands simple conversation and classroom discussion easily
Oral Fluency	Cannot carry on simple conversation	Carries on simple conversation very hesitantly	Carries on simple conversation and classroom discussion haltingly	Carries on simple conversation and classroom discussion nearly fluently	Carries on simple conversation and classroom discussion fluently and effortlessly
Vocabulary Skills	Cannot converse due to severe vocabulary limitations	Cannot make self understood due to considerable vocabulary limitations and misused words	Converses in a limited way due to inadequate vocabulary and misused words	Converses adequately by rephrasing often due to incomplete vocabulary	Converses fluently, using adequate vocabulary and idioms correctly
Pronunciation Mastery	Conversation is impossible due to severe pronunciation problems	Despite frequent repetition, conversation is severely limited by pronunciation difficulties	Conversation is often misunderstood due to pronunciation problems	Conversation is intelligible despite a detectable accent and intonation abnormalities	Conversation is natural and effortless due to accurate pronunciation and intonation
Oral Grammar	Conversation is impossible due to severe errors in grammar and word order	Conversation is limited to basic patterns of grammar and word order	Conversation is comprehensible despite frequent errors in grammar and word order	Conversation is understandable despite occasional errors in grammar and word order	Conversation is clear due to correct use of grammar and word order

© Harcourt

Group Summary Record Form

Students' Names	Listening Comprehension	Oral Fluency	Vocabulary Skills	Pronunciation Mastery	Oral Grammar	Comments

English-Language Learners Teacher's Guide

Sounds and Features of the English Language

Similarities across languages can result in ELLs' confusion with reading and spelling. The information on pages xviii–xxi describes some of the most common difficulties ELLs experience in learning English. Understanding where the problems and contrasts lie will give you an opportunity to bridge the gap between students' knowledge of their first languages and their success in English.

Problem Contrast	Chinese	French	Greek	Italian	Japanese	Korean	Spanish	Urdu	Vietnamese
/ā/-/a/			X	X	X	X		X	
/ā/-/e/			X	X	X	X	X	X	X
/a/-/e/	X		X	X	X	X	X	X	X
/a/-/o/	X	X	X	X	X	X	X	X	X
/a/-/u/	X		X	X	X		X	X	
/ē/-/i/	X	X	X	X	X	X	X	X	X
/e/-/u/	X		X	X			X	X	
/ō/-/o/	X		X	X	X		X	X	X
/o/-/ô/	X		X		X	X	X	X	X
/o/-/u/	X		X	X	X		X		X
/u/-/ōō/	X	X	X	X			X	X	X
/u/-/ŏŏ/	X		X		X		X		X
/u/-/ô/	X		X	X	X	X	X	X	
/ōō/-/ŏŏ/	X	X		X		X	X	X	
/b/-/p/	X					X	X		X
/b/-/v/			X		X	X	X		
/ch/-/j/				X		X	X		X
/ch/-/sh/	X	X	X		X	X	X		X
/d/-/th/	X			X	X	X	X	X	X
/f/-/th/				X		X	X	X	X
/l/-/r/	X				X	X	X		X
/n/-/ng/	X	X	X	X	X		X	X	
/s/-/sh/			X	X	X	X	X		X
/s/-/th/	X	X		X	X	X	X	X	X
/s/-/z/	X		X	X		X	X		X
/sh/-/th/				X	X	X	X	X	X
/t/-/th/	X			X	X	X	X	X	X
/th/-/th/	X	X		X	X	X	X	X	X
/th/-/z/	X	X	X	X	X	X	X	X	X

From *The ESL Teacher's Book of Lists*, ©1993 by The Center for Applied Research in Education

© Harcourt

Consonants

Initial Correspondences /b/b, /d/d, /p/p
Some LEP students, including speakers of Chinese, Samoan, and Korean, may have difficulty differentiating the initial sound of *bat* from the initial sound of *pat* and *dad*.

Initial Correspondences /f/f, /p/p, /v/v
Some LEP students, including speakers of Tagalog and Vietnamese, have difficulty differentiating the initial sound of *fat* from the initial sound of *pat* or *vat*. Students must be able to hear and produce these different sounds in order to become successful readers of English.

Initial Correspondence /v/v, /b/b
Spanish-speaking students may have difficulty differentiating the initial sound of *bat* from the initial sound of *vat*, since they are used to pronouncing /b/ when the letter *v* appears at the beginning of a word. In pronouncing English words that begin with *v*, these students often substitute /b/ for /v/; thus *vest* becomes *best*, and *very* becomes *berry*.

Initial Correspondences /j/j, /y/y, /ch/ch
The sound /j/ in *jar* is difficult for LEP students who often confuse or interchange this sound with /ch/ or /y/, causing major comprehension difficulties. In addition, Spanish has a similar sound /y/ that is often substituted for the sound /j/, resulting in confusion when students try to differentiate between the words *jam* and *yam*.

Initial correspondence /s/c, s
The letter-sound association for *c* usually follows the same generalizations in both English and Spanish. When *c* is followed by the letter *e* or *i*, it stands for the sound /s/; when *c* is followed by the letter *a*, *o*, or *u*, it stands for the sound /k/. In some Spanish dialects, when the letter *c* is followed by the letter *e* or *i*, the *c* stands for the sound /th/. Therefore, some Spanish-speaking students might have difficulty with this sound.

Initial Correspondence /s/s, /z/z
The sound /z/ is difficult for many LEP students to master because often it is not found in their native language. It is especially difficult for students to differentiate this sound from the sound /s/.

Initial Correspondence /n/n, kn; /l/l
The sound /n/ at the beginning of a word seems to present no special difficulties for most LEP students. However, students whose native language is Chinese, sometimes have difficulty differentiating this sound from the sound /l/ at the beginning of *lot*.

Initial Correspondence /r/r, wr; /l/l
Some LEP students, including speakers of Chinese, Japanese, Korean, Vietnamese, and Thai, may have great difficulty differentiating /r/ as in *rip* from /l/ as in *lip*. These students often pronounce both *lip* and *rip* with the beginning sound /l/.

Initial Correspondence /kw/qu, /w/w
Some LEP students have difficulty differentiating the initial sound /kw/ as in *queen* from the initial sound /w/ as in *wet*.

Initial Correspondence /v/v, /w/w
Some LEP students, including speakers of Chinese, Arabic, German, Samoan, and Thai, have difficulty differentiating /w/ as in *wet* from /v/ as in *van*. These students need much practice producing the sound /w/ in order to avoid confusing it with the sound /v/.

Initial Correspondence /g/g; /k/k,c
Some LEP students, especially speakers of Korean, Samoan, Vietnamese, Thai, and Indonesian, have difficulty differentiating /k/ as in *cat* and *king* from /g/ as in *go*. Speakers of Vietnamese and Thai especially have difficulty with these two sounds when they appear at the end of a word.

Initial Correspondence /h/h, /j/j, /hw/wh
Students who already read in Spanish may have difficulty with these sound-symbol correspondences, because in Spanish the letter *h* is silent. Students may forget to pronounce this sound in trying to decode

© Harcourt

English words, saying for example, /ot/ for *hot* and /at/ for *hat*. Because the sound /h/ is represented by the letter *j* in Spanish, this letter may be used in spelling English words that begin with *h*. Students may write *jat* for *hat, jot* for *hot, jouse* for *house*, and so on.

In addition, some LEP students may have difficulty differentiating the beginning sound of *hat* from the beginning sound of *what*. They will need practice in differentiating these two sounds.

Initial Correspondence /fr/fr, /fl/fl

The initial /fr/fr does not usually present difficulty for students who speak Spanish since these sounds are commonly found in Spanish. However, /fr/fr does present difficulty for students who speak Chinese or other Oriental languages, especially when differentiating /fr/fr from /fl/fl.

Initial Correspondences /gr/gr, /dr/dr, /br/br

Some LEP students, especially speakers of Chinese and Vietnamese, may have difficulty differentiating the initial sounds of *grass* from the initial sounds of *broom* and *dress*. Much practice is needed to help students hear and produce these sounds in English in order to avoid problems when they start to work with the written symbols that represent these sounds.

Initial Correspondences /th/th, /thr/thr, /t/t

Some LEP students, especially Spanish-speaking students, may have difficulty pronouncing words that begin with /th/ and /thr/, and differentiating these sounds from/t/. Much practice is needed to help students hear and produce these sounds in English in order to avoid problems when they start to work with the written symbols that represent these sounds.

Initial Correspondences /kr/cr, /kl/cl, /gl/gl

Some LEP students, especially speakers of Chinese or Vietnamese, may have difficulty with these clusters. These clusters do not present difficulty for Spanish-speaking students since they are commonly found in the Spanish language.

Initial Correspondences /skr/scr; /sk/sk,sc; /kr/cr

The intial consonant clusters /skr/*scr* and /sk/*sk,sc* may be difficult for LEP students of various language backgrounds. Spanish-speaking students have difficulty with the *s*-plus-consonant pronunciation. Speakers of other languages may have difficulty with the initial consonant cluster /kr/*cr*.

Initial Correspondences /st/st; /str/str; /sk/sk, sch, sc

The majority of LEP students, especially those who speak Spanish, have difficulty pronouncing these consonant clusters in the initial position. In Spanish, these clusters never appear at the beginning of a word. Thus students tend to add the /e/ sound in front of a word: *school* /sko͞ol/ becomes /esko͞ol/ and *street* is pronounced /estrēt/.

Initial Correspondences /tr/tr, /thr/thr, /t/t

The consonant clusters /tr/ and /thr/ are difficult for LEP students whose native languages do not have these sounds in combination. Some students have difficulty differentiating among /tr/, /thr/, /t/, and /t/ with the vowel *i*.

Initial Correspondences /sl/sl, /pl/pl

The consonant cluster *sl* presents some difficulty for Spanish-speaking students who are not used to encountering the *s*-plus-consonant sound at the beginning of words. These students often add the /e/ sound in front of a word; for example, *sleep* is pronounced /eslēp/. The /pl/ sound does not present difficulty for speakers of Spanish because it is common in Spanish. However, speakers of Chinese and Vietnamese, among others, may find it difficult to master.

Initial Correspondences /sp/sp, /sm/sm

The majority of LEP students have difficulty pronouncing the consonant clusters *sp* and *sm* in the initial position. In Spanish, these clusters never appear at the beginning of words. Often Spanish-speaking students add /e/ before the /s/; thus *spot* is pronounced /espot/.

© Harcourt

Initial Correspondences /sh/sh, /ch/ch

The sound /sh/ presents difficulty for many LEP students because it is not found in most languages. The sound /ch/ seems to be more common. Therefore many students do not distinguish between /sh/ and /ch/ and tend to substitute one for the other, saying *cheep* for *sheep* and *chin* for *shin*. This is particularly true of Spanish-speaking students.

Final Correspondences /p/p, /b/b

Spanish-speaking students may have difficulty hearing the final sound /p/ and may confuse this sound with the final sound /b/, since the final sound /b/ and /p/ do not often occur in Spanish.

Final Correspondences /t/t, /d/d

Some LEP students may have difficulty differentiating the final sound of *bat* from the final sound of *dad*. Much practice is needed to help students hear and produce these sounds in English to avoid problems when starting to work with the written symbols that represent these sounds.

Final Correspondences /ks/x; /s/s, ss

Final consonants can present a problem, especially for students whose native languages do not emphasize these consonants as much as English does. In Spanish, for example, there are only a few consonants that appear at the ends of words (*n,s,z,d,l,j*). Many Spanish-speaking people tend to drop the final consonant sound in conversation; for example, *reloj* becomes *relo*.

Final Correspondences /z/z, zz; /s/s, ss

The sound /z/ is difficult for many LEP students to master because often it is not found in their native languages. It is especially difficult for students to differentiate this sound from the sound /s/.

Final Correspondences /k/k, ck; /g/g

The final sound /g/ may be difficult for Spanish-speaking students since this sound never occurs at the end of Spanish words. Students may have difficulty hearing this sound and may pronounce it as the sound /k/ or omit the sound completely.

Final Correspondences /f/f, ff; /p/p

Some LEP students may have difficulty differentiating the final sound of *wife* from the final sound of *wipe*. Much practice is needed to help students hear and produce these sounds in English in order to avoid problems when they start to work with the written symbols that represent these sounds.

Final Correspondences /p/p, /t/t

Some LEP students may have difficulty differentiating the final sound of *ape* from that of *ate*. Much practice is needed to help students hear and produce these sounds in English in order to avoid problems when they start to work with the written symbols that represent these sounds.

Final Correspondences /d/d, /b/b

Some LEP students may have difficulty differentiating the final sound of *lad* from the final sound of *lab*. Much practice is needed to help students hear and produce these sounds in English in order to avoid problems when they start to work with the written symbols that represent these sounds.

Final Correspondences /ld/ld, nt/nt, nd/nd

Some LEP students may have difficulty differentiating the final sounds of *old* from those of *lint* and *find*. Two final consonant sounds increase the difficulty. Much practice is needed to help students hear and produce these sounds in English in order to avoid problems when they start to work with the written symbols that represent these sounds.

Final Correspondences /ng/ng, /ngk/nk

Some LEP students may have difficulty differentiating the final sounds of *sink* from the final sounds of *sing*. Much practice is needed to help students hear and produce these sounds in English in order to avoid problems when they start to work with the written symbols that represent these sounds.

Final Correspondences /s/s, ss; /st/st

Some LEP students may have difficulty differentiating the final sound of *gas* from the final sounds of *last*. Much practice is needed to help students hear and produce

© Harcourt

these sounds in English in order to avoid problems when they start to work with the written symbols that represent these sounds.

Final Correspondences /sh/sh; /ch/ch, tch
Some LEP students may have difficulty differentiating the final sound of *mush* from the final sound of *much*. Much practice is needed to help students hear and produce these sounds in English in order to avoid problems when they start to work with the written symbols that represent these sounds.

Final Correspondences /th/th, /t/t
Some LEP students, especially speakers of Spanish, may have difficulty differentiating the final sound of *bat* from the final sound of *bath*. Much practice is needed to help students hear and produce these sounds in English in order to avoid problems when they start to work with the written symbols that represent these sounds.

Vowels

Vowel Correspondences /a/a, /e/e
Short vowel sounds are the most difficult for LEP students to master. These create problems when students try to learn and apply the concept of rhyming. LEP students have difficulty differentiating the short vowel sound in *bat* from the short vowel sound in *bet*. Much practice is needed to help students hear and produce these sounds in English in order to avoid problems when they start to work with the written symbols that represent these sounds.

Vowel Correspondences /o/o, /u/u
The vowel sounds in *cot* and *cut* often cause great difficulty for students who speak Spanish, Chinese, Vietnamese, Tagalog, and Thai. These sounds must be practiced frequently.

Vowel Correspondences /i/i, /ē/ee, ea, e_e
Words with the short *i* vowel sound are difficult for speakers of Spanish, Chinese, Vietnamese, and Tagalog, among others. LEP students in general have difficulty pronouncing this sound as they tend to confuse it with the long *e* vowel sound.

Spanish-speaking students in particular have the tendency to replace the short *i* sound with the long *e* sound.

Vowel Correspondences /u/u, /a/a, /e/e
The vowel sound in *up* is one of the most difficult for LEP students to master because it does not exist in many languages and yet is one of the most common sounds in English. LEP students often have difficulty differentiating this sound from the vowel sounds in *bat* and *bet*. Much practice is needed to help students hear and produce these sounds in English in order to avoid problems when they start to work with the written symbols that represent these sounds.

Vowel Correspondences /o/o; /ō/oa, o_e; /ô/au, aw
The vowel sound in *cot* often causes great difficulty for LEP students who speak Spanish, Chinese, Vietnamese, Tagalog, or Thai. This sound must be practiced frequently, especially to differentiate it from the vowel sound in *coat* and *caught*. In addition, when the letters *oa* come together in Spanish, they stand for two separate sounds. Therefore, many Spanish-speaking students may have difficulty understanding that the letters *oa* can stand for one sound in English.

Vowel Correspondences /ā/a_e, /e/e
It is difficult for LEP students who speak Vietnamese, Spanish, or Tagalog to differentiate between the vowel sound in *race* and the vowel sound in *pet*. Much practice is needed to help students hear and produce these sounds in English in order to avoid problems when they start to work with the written symbols that represent these sounds.

Vowel Correspondences /ī/i_e, /a/a
The vowel sound in *bike* may present a problem for some LEP students who have difficulty differentiating this sound from the vowel sound in *bat*. Much practice is needed to help students hear and produce these sounds in English in order to avoid problems when they start to work with the written symbols that represent these sounds.

© Harcourt

LESSON 1

Use with "The Hot and Cold Summer"

Build Background/Access Prior Knowledge

Have students look at the illustrations on *Pupil Edition* pages 22–23. Tell students that the girl is a new neighbor of the boys. She wants to be their

Being a new neighbor makes me feel	because
nervous	I do not know anyone.
excited	I will meet new people.
sad	I miss my old friends.

friend. Ask students how they think the boys are treating the girl and how she feels. Then ask them to share their experiences of being a new neighbor to someone. Ask: **How do you feel when you are a new neighbor? Why do you feel this way?** Record the responses in a chart like the one shown.

Selection Vocabulary

PRETEACH Display Teaching Transparency 12 and read the words aloud. Then point to the pictures as you read the following sentences:

1. There was a **commotion** at the race! There was a lot of noise.
2. We were all **exhausted**. We were very tired.
3. I made a **vow** to teach Sammy to sit and stay. I promised my Mom I would train Sammy.
4. The trainer is an **authority** on dogs. He knows a lot about dogs.
5. We got a certificate as a **souvenir**. It will be a reminder of the class.
6. It's **incredible** how the training works! We can hardly believe how good the dog is now.

Selection Vocabulary

RETEACH Revisit Teaching Transparency 12. Read the words with students. Have students work in pairs to discuss the meanings of the words and to answer questions such as: *Does **commotion** mean "excitement" or "calm"?*

Write the following sentence frames on the board. Read each sentence and ask students to choose a vocabulary word to complete it. Write students' responses in the blanks.

1. I bought a postcard as a _____ of our field trip. (*souvenir*)
2. I was _____ after playing soccer all morning. (*exhausted*)
3. Nick made a _____ to finish his homework before dinner. (*vow*)
4. All the dogs barked and made a big _____. (*commotion*)
5. The sunset was _____. It filled the sky with color. (*incredible*)
6. Mr. Diaz is a language _____. He speaks three languages. (*authority*)

Have students write the vocabulary words in their Language Dictionaries.

FLUENCY PRACTICE For oral fluency, have students read the sentence frames aloud. Encourage them to describe the illustrations on Teaching Transparency 12 by using the vocabulary words and any other words they know.

BEFORE

Reading "The Hot and Cold Summer" pages 22–40

Build Background: "The Hot and Cold Summer"

Revisit the pictures on *Pupil Edition* pages 22–23. Tell students that the girl is Bolivia. Explain that Bolivia is visiting the boys' neighborhood for the summer. She wants to make friends with Rory and Derek. Ask students what they think Bolivia might do to become friends with the boys.

DISTANT VOYAGES

Focus Skill Prefixes, Suffixes, and Roots

PRETEACH Explain to students that a word part added to the beginning of a word is a *prefix*; a word part added to the end of a word is a *suffix*; a *root* is a word part that must be combined with other word parts to make a word. A *root word* can stand alone. Draw two three-column charts on the board: one with the headings *Prefix*, *Root or Root Word*, and *New Word*; the other with the headings *Root or Root Word*, *Suffix*, and *New Word*. Tell students that the word *visitor* is a root word combined with a suffix. Write the word parts and the word *visitor* on the second chart. Continue to fill in the charts with words from the selection after students have read the story.

AFTER

Reading "The Hot and Cold Summer"

Directed Reading: "The Hot and Cold Summer"

RETEACH Use the sentences below to walk students through the story.

Pages 22–25
Pages 26–29

- This is Bolivia. She is visiting the boys' neighborhood for the summer.
- Here are Rory and Derek. They don't want to meet Bolivia.
- The neighbors are having a barbecue to welcome Bolivia.
- Bolivia tries to talk to Rory and Derek, but the boys have made a vow not to talk to her.
- This is a cake for Bolivia.
- Are the boys excited to have a new friend? (*no*)

QUESTIONS: pages 22–29

- Who is visiting the boys' neighborhood for the summer? (*Bolivia*)
- Why do the boys keep their mouths full of food? (*so they can't speak to Bolivia*)

Pages 30–35

- Derek and Rory are on their bikes.
- Bolivia is calling to them from the window. How does she look? (*upset*)
- Here is a parrot flying up into a tree. Her name is Lucette.
- Neighbors are running to the tree. One of them has a ladder.
- The boys are running to the tree, too. Everyone wants to catch Lucette.

Pages 36–40

- One of the boys is holding up a radio so Lucette can hear it.
- The man on the ladder gets Lucette, and Bolivia is happy.
- Lucette is on Bolivia's shoulder. One of the boys is talking to Bolivia.

QUESTIONS: pages 30–40

- Is Lucette Bolivia's baby sister? (*no*)
- What does Derek hold up for Lucette to hear? (*radio*)
- Who came to help Bolivia get Lucette back? (*neighbors, fire department, Rory, Derek*)

FLUENCY PRACTICE Ask volunteers to read aloud some of the dialogue on *Pupil Edition* page 35. Encourage students to describe the illustration on page 34. Encourage students to use the vocabulary words in their descriptions.

Build Background: "MINE"

PRETEACH Remind students that in "The Hot and Cold Summer," they read about a girl who visits a new neighborhood. In "MINE" they will read about a boy who moves to a new place and writes about it. Ask students what they would write about if they moved to a new place.

English-Language Learners Book

Write these words on the board and use them in sentences to illustrate their meanings.

- I write my name on the cover of my **notebook**.
- There are many new **words** for me to learn in English.
- My first **language** is Spanish.
- Ming is our **neighbor** who lives next door.
- She is my new **friend**.
- The **author** of my favorite book visited our class.

Have students add the concept words to their Language Dictionaries.

Concept Words
notebook
words
language
neighbor
friend
author

Directed Reading: "MINE"

📖 **Summary** *A boy new to the United States writes his thoughts in a notebook. Everything around him seems strange and difficult, especially English. Eventually he makes friends and discovers the public library.*

Use these bulleted sentences to walk students through the story.

Pages 2–3
- This notebook belongs to the boy. He wrote the word *MINE* on it.
- The boy is in a new school. He doesn't feel comfortable there.

Pages 4–7
- Look at what the boy writes.
- The boy asks his mother if he can play outside.

Pages 8–9
- The class is singing a song.
- The boy doesn't know the words to the song, but he wants to learn them.

❓ QUESTIONS: pages 2–9
- Does the boy feel comfortable at school? (*no*)
- What did the boy's mother give him? (*a notebook*)
- What does the boy ask his mother? (*if he can go outside*)

Pages 10–11
- The boy meets other people who are new to the United States.
- Not all of his neighbors speak English. Some speak other languages.

Pages 12–16
- An author visits the boy's class. She writes books in Spanish and in English.
- The boy is eating lunch with his new friends.
- The boy is going to his favorite place, the public library, to read books.

❓ QUESTIONS: pages 10–16
- Does the boy meet other people who are new to the United States? (*yes*)
- What special new place does the boy find? (*He finds the public library.*)

⭐ (Focus Skill) Prefixes, Suffixes, and Roots

RETEACH Review prefixes, suffixes, roots, and root words with students. Then draw on the board two three-column charts like the ones you created in the Preteach activity. Ask students to revisit the story to complete at least one row in each chart.

FLUENCY PRACTICE Ask students to read aloud one of the notebook entries from "MINE." Then have students use the illustration on pages 12–13 to retell part of the story.

Shared Writing: Narrative Paragraph

PRETEACH Tell students that they are going to work with you to write a paragraph retelling "The Hot and Cold Summer." Ask students to generate a list of story events to include, and write the list on the board.

Ask students if they have listed all the important events. Then ask them if the events are in the correct sequence. Add and reorder events as needed. Finally, write the sentences in paragraph form on the board with the help of students.

1. Derek and Rory decide not to be Bolivia's friend.
2. Bolivia comes to the barbecue and tries to talk to the boys.
3. Lucette escapes as Derek and Rory ride by.
4. All the neighbors, including Derek and Rory, try to catch Lucette.
5. The boys help catch Lucette and then talk to Bolivia.

Grammar: Declarative and Interrogative Sentences

PRETEACH Discuss declarative and interrogative sentences with students. Point out the following:
- A sentence expresses a complete thought.
- A **declarative sentence** makes a statement and ends with a period.
- An **interrogative sentence** asks a question and ends with a question mark.

Write the following sentences on the board and read them aloud:
- *Lucette flies out the window.*
- *Where does she go?*
- *She lands in a tree.*

Tell students that the first and the third sentences are declarative sentences; they make statements. The second sentence is an interrogative sentence; it asks a question. Point out that the first and third sentences end with periods, and the second sentence ends with a question mark.

Read the following items aloud. Ask students to say whether each sentence is a declarative sentence or an interrogative sentence.
1. Will Bolivia be staying a long time? (*interrogative*)
2. Bolivia's parrot is named Lucette. (*declarative*)
3. Do you think that the boys will be her friends? (*interrogative*)
4. I think they will decide to be her friends. (*declarative*)
5. The boys decide that Bolivia is interesting after all. (*declarative*)

FLUENCY PRACTICE Have volunteers read aloud the paragraph they completed in the writing activity.

Shared Writing: Descriptive Paragraph

`RETEACH` Display the completed paragraph from the Preteach activity. Read it aloud with students. Ask them if they would make any changes in it and why. Discuss students' suggestions for revising the paragraph. Write a revised paragraph based on students' suggestions. Then have students copy the revised paragraph into their Language Journals. Encourage students to personalize their paragraphs.

Grammar-Writing Connection

`RETEACH` Write these sentences on the board, and read them aloud with students: *Bolivia was visiting a new neighborhood for the summer. The boy in "MINE" had moved to a new place.*

Have students work in pairs or in a small group to discuss how it feels to visit or move to a new place. Then have students draw pictures to show their ideas. Encourage students to describe their pictures orally. Then work with them to write a declarative sentence that describes each picture. Remind students that a declarative sentence makes a statement and ends with a period. Check students' writing and suggest any corrections they need to make.

FLUENCY PRACTICE Have students choose a favorite notebook entry from "MINE" to read aloud.

Name _____

Think about the paragraph you wrote to retell "The Hot and Cold Summer." Draw a picture to go with the paragraph. Make up your own title, and write it above your picture.

_____

TO THE TEACHER Model for students
sequencing a set of events in time order.

The Hot and Cold Summer/MINE • Lesson 1 7

© Harcourt

LESSON 2

Use with "Sees Behind Trees"

BEFORE

Building Background and Vocabulary

Build Background/Access Prior Knowledge

Have students look at the illustrations on *Pupil Edition* pages 50–51. Tell students that the boy is learning to shoot arrows for a contest. Then ask students to share their experiences with tests of physical skill. Ask: **How do you feel when you compete in a game or sport? Why?** Record the responses in a chart like the one shown.

Competing in a game or sport makes me feel	because I
nervous	know everyone is watching.
sick	am not very good.
afraid	think people might make fun of me.

Selection Vocabulary

PRETEACH Display Teaching Transparency 19 and read the words aloud. Then point to the pictures as you read the following sentences:

1. Soft, green **moss** grows on the tree.
2. After the chase ended, the rabbit tried to **compose** itself.
3. The rabbit hears the **tread** of the boy's moccasins. It hears the sound of his footsteps.
4. The man **sternly** tells the boy to be quiet. The man speaks harshly.
5. A **quiver** holds the boy's arrows.
6. Did the boy **exaggerate** about his fear of the contest? Was his fear greater than it needed to be?

AFTER

Building Background and Vocabulary

Selection Vocabulary

RETEACH Revisit Teaching Transparency 19. Read the words with students. Have students work in pairs to discuss the meanings of the words and to answer questions such as: *Is **moss** a plant or an animal?*

Write the following sentence frames on the board. Read each frame and ask students to choose a vocabulary word to complete it. Write students' responses in the blanks.

1. The man _____ yelled at us to stop. (*sternly*)
2. Some people do _____ when they talk about their fear of spiders. (*exaggerate*)
3. _____ grew on the rocks by the river. (*Moss*)
4. After the excitement, the woman tried to _____ herself. (*compose*)
5. The boy took an arrow from his _____. (*quiver*)
6. She hears the _____ of boots on the porch. (*tread*)

Have students write the vocabulary words in their Language Dictionaries.

FLUENCY PRACTICE Have students read the completed sentence frames aloud. Encourage them to describe the illustrations on Teaching Transparency 19 by using the vocabulary words and any other words they know.

8 Lesson 2 • *English-Language Learners Teacher's Guide*

Build Background: "Sees Behind Trees"

Revisit the pictures on *Pupil Edition* pages 50–51. Tell students that the boy is Walnut, the story's main character. Walnut is practicing for a contest in which he will shoot arrows. Walnut must do well in the contest to be recognized as a man in his village. Discuss with students how he might feel while preparing for the contest. (*nervous, afraid, anxious*)

DISTANT
VOYAGES

 Narrative Elements

PRETEACH Tell students that the narrative elements of a story are plot, setting, and characters. Explain that the plot is the sequence of events that make up the story's action. A plot centers around a main problem and how it is resolved. Draw on the board a three-column chart labeled *Problem*, *Actions*, and *Solution*.

Tell students that the main problem in this story is Walnut's fear that he will not become a man because he cannot shoot an arrow well. Write this problem on the chart. After reading, ask students to identify what actions are taken to solve the problem and how the problem is finally solved. Record the students' responses in the chart.

Directed Reading: "Sees Behind Trees"

RETEACH Use these sentences to walk students through the story.

- This is Walnut and his mother in the forest. The forest is the story's setting.
- Walnut's mother throws moss, and he tries to hit it with his arrow.
- Walnut misses the moss.
- Walnut tells his uncle that he cannot hit a target with his arrow. This is the main problem in this story.

- Walnut is in the forest again. He wears a blindfold that covers his eyes.
- Walnut is learning to listen to the sounds in the forest.

- Is Walnut good at shooting his bow and arrow? (*no*)
- What is the target that Walnut tries to hit? (*moss*)
- What does Walnut listen to in the forest? (*He listens to the sounds.*)

- Walnut, his uncle, and his father are talking about the contest.
- The boys have their arrows in their quivers as they walk to the contest.
- The village leader says that there will be a new contest before the shooting contest.

- Walnut puts the blindfold on and describes what he "sees" with his ears. He wins the contest.
- Walnut is recognized as a man, and he gets a new name, Sees Behind Trees.

- Does Walnut go to the contest? (*yes*)
- Who else is in the contest? (*other boys*)
- What does Walnut do to get his new name? (*He "sees" with his ears.*)

FLUENCY PRACTICE Encourage students to describe the illustration on *Pupil Edition* pages 58–59. Suggest students use the vocabulary words in their descriptions.

BEFORE

Making
Connections
pages 66–67

Concept Words
throw
catch
practice
learn
close
miss

AFTER

Skill Review
pages 68–69

Build Background: "The Test"

PRETEACH Remind students that "Sees Behind Trees" is about a boy who practices for an important contest. In "The Test" they will read about Tom, a boy who has to take a gym test that he is afraid of failing.

English-
Language
Learners
Book

Write the concept words on the board, and use them in sentences to illustrate their meanings.

- I will **throw** the ball to you and you will **catch** it.
- If you **practice**, you can **learn** to hit a ball.
- Don't **close** your eyes before you swing. Keep them open.
- If you do not watch the ball, you will **miss** it.

Have students add the concept words to their Language Dictionaries.

Directed Reading: "The Test"

📖 **Summary** *Fifth-grader Tom is not good at sports, and he has to take a gym test. Tom's teacher tells him about the test that Mr. Otero, the gym teacher, will give him. Mr. Otero helps Tom solve his problem.*

Use these bulleted sentences to walk students through the story.

Pages 2–3
- This is Tom and his teacher, Ms. Green. Tom's stomach hurts because he has to take a gym test.

Pages 4–7
- Ms. Green explains that Tom will catch, throw, and kick a ball during the test.
- Tom is afraid that he will fail the test or get hurt.
- Tom wants to take the test next week, but he has to take it today.
- Here is the gym teacher, Mr. Otero. Tom tells him that his stomach hurts.
- Tom tells the gym teacher his arm hurts and that he cannot throw the ball.

❓ QUESTIONS:
pages 2–7
- Does Tom have a stomachache? (*yes*)
- Who is Mr. Otero? (*the gym teacher*)
- How does Tom feel about taking the test? (*He doesn't want to take it*)

Pages 8–12
- Mr. Otero shows Tom how to catch a ball. Tom catches it!
- Tom tries to throw a ball to Mr. Otero, but it goes over Mr. Otero's head.
- Mr. Otero shows Tom how to throw a ball. Tom throws the ball right to Mr. Otero.

Pages 13–16
- Mr. Otero asks Tom to kick a ball, but Tom misses it because he closes his eyes.
- Mr. Otero tells Tom to keep his eyes open and kick the ball. Tom does it.
- Mr. Otero tells Tom that he can run, throw, catch, and kick.
- Tom's stomachache is gone. He passed the test!

❓ QUESTIONS:
pages 8–16
- Does Mr. Otero help Tom solve his problem? (*yes*)
- What does Tom do with his eyes the first time he tries to kick? (*closes them*)
- Why is Tom happy at the end of the story? (*He passed the test.*)

(Focus Skill) Narrative Elements

RETEACH Review with students the narrative elements, focusing on the main problem. On the board, draw a three-column chart like the one you created for "Sees Behind the Trees." Ask students to revisit "The Test" to find story details to complete the chart.

FLUENCY PRACTICE Have students use the illustration on page 14 to retell part of "The Test." Encourage them to use as many concept words as possible.

Shared Writing: Descriptive Paragraph

PRETEACH Tell students that they are going to work with you to write a descriptive paragraph about a baseball game. On the board, draw a senses chart like the one shown. Brainstorm with students words and phrases to add to the chart, such as *cheering*, *national anthem*, *crack of bat hitting ball* for the Hear column.

See	Hear	Touch	Taste	Smell

Write the following sentence frames on the board or on chart paper. Read each sentence with students and ask them to use words and phrases from the chart to complete it. As you write each response in the blank, have students write it on their lap boards.

> It was the last game of the season. The Redbirds were playing the Bluebirds for the championship. The weather was _____. All around me, I saw _____. The smell of _____ and _____ filled the air. I heard the sounds of _____. The bleachers were _____, but my _____ tasted _____. One batter hit the ball very far. It was a home run! Don't count the Bluebirds out, though. They could win next year!

Grammar: Imperative and Exclamatory Sentences

PRETEACH Discuss imperative and exclamatory sentences with students. Point out the following:

- An **imperative sentence** gives a command or makes a request. The subject is *you* (understood).
- An **exclamatory sentence** expresses strong feeling. It ends with an exclamation point.

Write these sentences on the board and read them aloud:

- *It was a home run!*
- *Don't count the Bluebirds out, though.*
- *They could win next year!*

Tell students that the first and third sentences are exclamatory sentences, and the second sentence is an imperative sentence.

Point out that an imperative sentence also may be an exclamatory sentence. Write an example, such as, "Run to second base!"

Read the numbered sentences aloud. Ask students to say whether each is an imperative sentence, an exclamatory sentence, or both.

1. Please buy me some popcorn. (*imperative*)
2. We won! (*exclamatory*)
3. Don't swing if the pitch is too low. (*imperative*)
4. Sit next to me. (*imperative*)
5. Don't strike out! (*imperative and exclamatory*)

FLUENCY PRACTICE Have volunteers read aloud the descriptive paragraph they completed in the writing activity.

Shared Writing: Descriptive Paragraph

RETEACH Display the completed paragraph from the Preteach activity. Read it aloud with students. Ask students what they would like to add. Discuss students' suggestions for additions to the paragraph. Write a revised paragraph based on students' suggestions. Then have students copy the revised paragraph into their Language Journals. Encourage students to personalize their paragraphs by adding even more details.

Grammar-Writing Connection

RETEACH Write these sentences on the board and read them aloud with students: *Walnut had to pass an important test, and he was very worried. Tom also was very worried about the test he had to take. In the end, both Walnut and Tom did well on their tests.*

Have students work in pairs or in a small group to discuss what advice they would give to someone who was worried about a big test. Then have students draw a picture to show their ideas. Encourage students to describe their pictures orally. Then work with students to write imperative sentences that tell their advice. Remind students that an imperative sentence gives a command or makes a request and has the (understood) subject *you*. Check students' writing and suggest any corrections they need to make.

FLUENCY PRACTICE Have students choose a favorite paragraph or page from "The Test" to read aloud.

Name _____

Use the spaces below to draw a comic strip. Use pictures and words to retell the story "The Test." Be sure to show Tom's problem and how he solves it. Use another sheet of paper if you need more room.

TO THE TEACHER Model for students how to use speech balloons for characters' words and thought balloons for thoughts.

Sees Behind Trees/The Test • Lesson 2   13

LESSON 3

Use with **"Yang the Third and Her Impossible Family"**

BEFORE
Building Background and Vocabulary

Build Background/Access Prior Knowledge

Discuss with students the concept of family. Ask them to share their experiences and feelings about their families. Ask: **What are some good things about having a family? What are some hard things about being part of a family?** Record students' responses in a chart like the one shown.

Good Things	Hard Things
Families do nice things for you.	You have to share.
Families are fun to do things with.	You do not always get to do what you want.
Family members can teach you things.	Family members may upset you.

Selection Vocabulary

PRETEACH Display Teaching Transparency 28 and read the words aloud. Point to the appropriate picture parts as you read these sentences:
1. the violinist practiced for his **audition**. He wanted to be hired to play in the orchestra.
2. A woman was his **accompanist**. She played along with him.
3. They played **simultaneously**. They played at the same time.
4. They played a **sonata**. A sonata is a piece of music with three or four parts.
5. He **grimaced** when he made a mistake. He made an unhappy face.
6. He thanked her for her **accompaniment**. He thanked her for playing the sonata with him.

AFTER
Building Background and Vocabulary

Selection Vocabulary

RETEACH Revisit Teaching Transparency 28. Read the words with students. Have students work in pairs to discuss the meanings of the words and to answer questions such as: *Is a **sonata** a kind of music or a kind of instrument?*

Write the following sentence frames on the board. Read each sentence and ask students to choose a vocabulary word to complete it. Write students' responses in the blanks.
1. Teresita and her _____ played well. (*accompanist*)
2. Carlos played a _____ on the piano. (*sonata*)
3. I played the viola, and she provided the _____. (*accompaniment*)
4. I _____ when I dropped my sheet music. (*grimaced*)
5. We all bowed _____. (*simultaneously*)
6. the music students hoped to do as well at their next _____. (*audition*)

Have students write the selection vocabulary words in their Language Dictionaries.

FLUENCY PRACTICE Encourage students to describe the illustrations on Teaching Transparency 28 by using the vocabulary words.

14 Lesson 3 • *English-Language Learners Teacher's Guide*

Build Background: "Yang the Third and Her Impossible Family"

DISTANT VOYAGES

Read the title aloud to students and have them look at the cover illustration. Tell students that the girl is Yingmei, or Mary, the main character in this story. Discuss with students possible reasons why Mary finds her family "impossible." (*Maybe they embarrass her, or maybe she has to share or do things she doesn't want to do.*)

 Prefixes, Suffixes, and Roots

PRETEACH Tell students that when a prefix or a suffix is added to a root word, it changes the meaning of the root word. Draw on the board a three-column chart with the headings *Prefix or Suffix*, *Meaning*, and *Story Examples*. Tell students that *im-* is a prefix that is added to the root word *possible*, and ask them how *im-* changes the meaning of the root word. (*It adds the meaning "not."*) Fill in the first row of the chart.

After students have read the story, have them find words from the story to add to the chart.

Directed Reading: "Yang the Third and Her Impossible Family"

RETEACH Use the sentences to walk students through the story.

Page 73
- This is Yingmei Yang. She likes to be called Mary. She is also called Third Sister because she was the third child born in her family.

Pages 74–77
- Mary and her family are from China.
- Mary plays the cello. Her friend Holly plays the viola.
- Holly has a tryout on Wednesday, but her accompanist is sick. Holly needs someone to play piano for her.
- Mary says that her mother, a pianist, could play.

QUESTIONS: pages 73–77
- Are Mary and Holly friends? (*yes*)
- What instrument does Mary's mother play? (*piano*)
- Why does Holly need an accompanist? (*She has a tryout.*)

Pages 78–80
- Holly comes to Mary's house so that Holly can practice with Mary's mother.
- Mary's family listens as Holly and Mary's mother play.
- Mary's mother plays well, but Holly does not.

Pages 81–84
- Holly's mother misunderstands what the Yangs say about the tryout.
- Mary sees that Holly and her mother are unhappy, so she follows them out.
- Mary learns that the misunderstanding happened because of language differences.
- Mary plans to write what she learned from the misunderstanding.

QUESTIONS: pages 78–84
- Does Mary's mother play the piano well? (*yes*)
- What kind of music do Holly and Mary's mother play together? (*a sonata*)
- Why does Mary follow Holly and her mother when they leave? (*She can see that something is wrong.*)

FLUENCY PRACTICE Have students describe the illustration on *Pupil Edition* page 81, using as many vocabulary words as they can.

Making Connections
pages 86–87

Build Background: "Are We Having Fun Yet?"

PRETEACH Remind students that "Yang the Third and Her Impossible Family" is about a girl who is embarrassed by her family. Point out that "Are We Having Fun Yet?" is about a girl who goes on a trip with her family. Ask students what problems a family might have on a long car trip.

English-Language Learners Book

Concept Words
trip
carry
beach
boat
lost

Write the concept words on the board, and use them in sentences to illustrate their meanings.

- We took a **trip** to California.
- We all had to **carry** our own bags.
- We went swimming at the **beach**.
- We went fishing on a **boat**.
- I **lost** my hat in the ocean.

Have students add these concept words to their Language Dictionaries.

Skill Review
pages 88–89

Directed Reading: "Are We Having Fun Yet?"

 Summary *Ana and her family take a car trip to Florida. Everyone becomes tired and crabby. Ana sees a lost dog. Ana's parents say that she cannot keep the dog, but in the end they let her take him home.*

Use these bulleted sentences to walk students through the story.

Pages 2–5
- This is Ana. She and her family are going to Florida to visit relatives.
- Ana wants to take her stuffed animals, but she is told to take only one.
- On the long drive to Florida, Ana's family gets lost, and the car has a flat tire.
- By the time they get to Florida, everyone is tired and crabby.

Pages 6–9
- Ana and her cousin, Ernesto, see a lost dog and feed it. Ana names it Sammy.
- Ana's papa and grandfather think that feeding the dog is a bad idea.

QUESTIONS: pages 2–9
- Do Ana and her family go to Florida? (*yes*)
- After the car is unloaded, what does Ana see? (*a dog*)

Pages 10–16
- Ana and her father are having fun at the beach.
- Back at Ana's uncle's house, they see the dog, Sammy, again.
- Papa says the dog is cute, but Mama says Ana cannot keep him.
- Papa and Uncle Emilio feed and play with Sammy and let him in the house.
- Papa says they are not taking the dog home, but Mama says it is all right.
- Ana goes to a carnival with her relatives. When they come home, Sammy is in Mama's lap. Ana's parents let her take Sammy home.

QUESTIONS: pages 10–16
- Does Sammy become Ana's dog? (*yes*)
- Why is Ana happy at the end of the story? (*Her parents let her keep Sammy.*)

(Focus Skill) Prefixes, Suffixes, and Roots

RETEACH Review prefixes, suffixes, and root words with students. Then draw on the board a three-column chart like the one you created for the story "Yang the Third and Her Impossible Family." Ask students to revisit "Are We Having Fun Yet?" to complete the chart.

FLUENCY PRACTICE Ask students to read aloud a favorite passage from the story "Are We Having Fun Yet?"

Shared Writing: Realistic Story

PRETEACH Tell students that they are going to
work with you to write a fictional story about
something that happens to a family on a long trip.

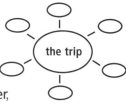

On the board, list at least five characters—all family
members—who could be in the story. For each character,
have students suggest a name and a brief description.

Next, draw a web with "the trip" in the center circle. Have students add at
least five problems that could happen on the trip around the web's center.

Have students choose a main character and a main problem for the story.
Elicit ideas for the resolution of the problem as well. Prompt students to
dictate sentences for the story. For example, ask: **How will the family
travel?** (*on an airplane*) **Where are they going?** (*to Los Angeles*) Then ask:
How will we say that in the story? (*Gloria and her family are taking an
airplane trip to Los Angeles.*)

Work with students to combine the generated story problems, characters,
problem resolution, and sentences into a realistic story. Write a draft of
the story on the board.

Grammar: Simple and Complete Subjects

PRETEACH Discuss complete and simple subjects with students. Point out
the following:
- Every sentence has a subject that tells who or what the sentence is about.
- The **complete subject** includes all the words that tell who or what the sen-
  tence is about.
- The **simple subject** is the main word or words in the complete subject.

Write the following sentences on the board and read them aloud:
- *The huge silver airplane gleamed in the sun.*
- *Gloria's baby brother cried loudly in her ear.*
- *Gloria heard the pilot say something.*

Point out the complete subject and the simple subject in each sentence.

Read the following items aloud. Ask students to identify the complete
subject and the simple subject in each sentence.
1. The plane's engines roared. (*The plane's engine; engine*)
2. Gloria's father told her to fasten her seatbelt. (*Gloria's father; father*)
3. The plane took off. (*The plane; plane*)
4. The flight attendant offered Gloria some juice. (*The flight attendant;
   attendant*)
5. Gloria wondered if the baby would cry all the way to Los Angeles.
   (*Gloria; Gloria*)

FLUENCY PRACTICE Have volunteers read aloud the stories they drafted in
the writing activity.

Shared Writing: Realistic Story

RETEACH Display the completed story from the Preteach activity. Read it aloud with students. Ask students what changes they would like to make. Discuss students' suggestions for changes or additions to the story. Write the revised story based on students' suggestions. Then have students copy the revised story into their Language Journals. Encourage students to personalize their stories.

Grammar-Writing Connection

RETEACH Write these sentences on the board and read them aloud with students: *Mary was often embarrassed by her family. Ana had struggles with her family on the trip to Florida.*

Have students work in pairs or in a small group to discuss how it feels to have problems with family members. Then have students draw pictures to show their ideas. Encourage students to describe their pictures orally. Work with them to write a sentence that describes each picture and to label the complete subject and the simple subject. Check students' work and suggest any corrections they need to make.

FLUENCY PRACTICE Have students choose a favorite part of "Are We Having Fun Yet?" to read aloud.

Imagine that you are Ana. Imagine that you have just returned from the boat ride. Write a postcard to your best friend, Celia. Tell her about your trip so far. Write your postcard on the lines below. Draw a picture for Celia at the bottom of the page.

TO THE TEACHER Model for students how to address a postcard.

Yang the Third and Her Impossible Family/Are We Having Fun Yet? • **Lesson 3** **19**

© Harcourt

Use with "Dear Mrs. Parks"

Build Background/Access Prior Knowledge

Discuss with students the importance of learning. Encourage
them to share their experiences
with learning. Ask: **What things
have you learned already that help you in life? What things will you
need to learn to help you in the future?** List students' responses in a
chart on the board similar to the one given.

Already Learned	Will Need to Learn
how to talk	how to do a job
how to use a computer	how to drive a car
how to ride a bike	how to take care of a home

Selection Vocabulary

PRETEACH Display Teaching Transparency 37 and read the words aloud.
Then point to the pictures as you read the following sentences:

1. She has lots of **correspondence** to read. She has many letters.
2. Other students **ridiculed** her. They made fun of her.
3. But she kept her **dignity**. She stayed calm and poised.
4. He is her **mentor**. He is a wise teacher.
5. He likes to **counsel** students. He likes to give them advice.
6. She has the **potential** to be a doctor. She may be a doctor someday.
7. She reads about women who **inspire** her. Their stories her try to do
   her best.

Selection Vocabulary

RETEACH Revisit Teaching Transparency 37. Read the words with
students. Have students work in pairs to discuss the meanings of the
words and to answer questions such as: *Does **correspondence** mean
"trash" or "letters"? Is a **mentor** a "teacher" or a "student"?*

Write the following sentence frames on the board. Read each sentence
and ask students to choose a vocabulary word to complete it. Write
students' responses in the blanks.

1. People who are different are often _____. (*ridiculed*)
2. My dad is my _____. (*mentor*)
3. Grandmother speaks clearly and with _____. (*dignity*)
4. He always answers his _____. (*correspondence*)
5. Beautiful songs _____ me to sing. (*inspire*)
6. I like to play, but my teachers _____ me to study. (*counsel*)
7. I have the _____ to be a doctor. (*potential*)

Have students write the selection vocabulary words in their Language
Dictionaries.

FLUENCY PRACTICE Have students read the sentence frames aloud.
Encourage them to describe the illustrations on Teaching Transparency 37 by
using the vocabulary words and any other words they know.

Build Background: "Dear Mrs. Parks"

Show students the cover of "Dear Mrs. Parks" and the photos of Rosa Parks, Martin Luther King, Jr., and Jesse Jackson. Explain who Mrs. Parks is. Tell students that many children write letters to her and that they will read some of the letters and Mrs. Parks's answers.

DISTANT VOYAGES

Making Judgments

PRETEACH Tell students that making judgments means making decisions based on evidence. Then draw a diagram on the board with a large box at the top labeled *Judgment* and, beneath it, three smaller boxes labeled *Evidence*. Tell students that Mrs. Parks believes that learning is important throughout life. Explain that this is a judgment that can be made based on evidence in the story, and write the judgment on the chart. After students have read the story have them find examples of evidence from the story which support the judgment. Record the examples on the chart.

Pages 92–95

Pages 96–97

❓ QUESTIONS:
pages 92–97

Pages 98–99

Pages 100–104

❓ QUESTIONS:
pages 98–104

Directed Reading: "Dear Mrs. Parks"

RETEACH Use these sentences to walk students through the story.

- This is Rosa Parks, a hero of the American civil rights movement.
- Here is Mrs. Parks with Martin Luther King, Jr.
- These are letters that two boys wrote to Mrs. Parks.
- These are the answers that Mrs. Parks wrote to the boys. She wrote about asking questions and learning new things.
- This picture shows students raising their hands to ask questions.
- These are postmarks on envelopes.
- Does Mrs. Parks answer the letters she receives? (*yes*)
- Who writes letters to Mrs. Parks? (*students*)
- Who is Mrs. Parks? (*She is a hero of the civil rights movement.*)
- As a child, Mrs. Parks was too sick to go to school and had to learn at home.
- Mrs. Parks's grandmother was her main teacher when she was young.
- This picture shows an older woman. In the letter, a girl named Adrienne asks about the "old days."
- This picture shows part of an American flag. In the letter, a boy named Michael asks about changes that Mrs. Parks has seen in the last 50 years.
- Mrs. Parks tells Michael about changes that have taken place in America.
- This last letter is from a boy named Larry.
- Did Mrs. Parks go to school when she was a young girl? (*no*)
- Who was Mrs. Parks' main teacher when she was young? (*her grandmother*)
- In your judgment, was her grandmother a good teacher? What evidence supports your judgment? (*Accept reasonable responses*)
- What things do students ask Mrs. Parks about? (*the "old days," changes*)

FLUENCY PRACTICE Ask volunteers to describe the illustration on *Pupil Edition* pages 100–101. Encourage students to use vocabulary words in their descriptions.

Build Background: "What You Can Learn, What You Can Do"

English-Language Learners Book

PRETEACH Remind students that in "Dear Mrs. Parks," Mrs. Parks counseled students in her letters that it is important to learn. In "What You Can Learn, What You Can Do," students will read about the importance of different school subjects.

Concept Words
subjects
jobs
skills
interview
learn
measure

Write the concept words on the board and use them in sentences to illustrate their meanings.

- In school we study many **subjects**.
- Some **jobs** are more difficult than others. Some jobs require many **skills**.
- Mom had a job **interview** today.
- I will **learn** to make a cake. I will **measure** the correct amount of flour.

Have students add the concept words to their Language Dictionaries.

Directed Reading: "What You Can Learn, What You Can Do"

 Summary *The story "What You Can Learn, What You Can Do" tells why each school subject is important. It tells about jobs that use skills learned in social studies, language arts, math, science, and gym.*

Use these bulleted sentences to walk students through the story.

Pages 2–9
- This mail carrier works for the government. You study government in social studies.
- In language arts you learn how to read, write, and speak well. These are important skills for most jobs.
- In math you learn to work with numbers. This bank teller counts money.
- The carpenter and the cook must measure correctly.

QUESTIONS: pages 2–9
- Are reading, writing, and speaking things you learn in language arts? (*yes*)
- In what subject do you learn about government? (*social studies*)
- In which jobs do people use math skills? (*bank teller, carpenter, cook*)

Pages 10–16
- In science you learn about the Earth, plants, animals, and more.
- Farmers and veterinarians (doctors for animals) need to know science.
- In gym class you learn about being part of a team. You also learn skills you will need if you want to be an athlete or a referee.
- All the subjects you study in school will help you at your job and in your life.

QUESTIONS: pages 10–16
- Do doctors and nurses need to know science? (*yes*)
- What do you study in science? (*Earth, plants, animals, space*)

Making Judgments

RETEACH Review with students what it means to make judgments. Then draw on the board a diagram similar to the one you drew for the Preteach activity. In the *Judgment* box write *Language arts skills are important*. Ask students to revisit the story to find examples of evidence to support the judgement and to complete the chart.

FLUENCY PRACTICE Ask students to use the illustration on page 6 to retell part of the selection. Encourage them to use concept words in their retellings.

Interactive Writing: Personal Narrative

PRETEACH Tell students that they are going to work with you to write a personal narrative about learning something important. Ask students to share possible topics for narratives, and list them on the board.

> 1. learning to ride a bike
> 2. learning to take care of a puppy or kitten
> 3. learning to speak English
> 4. learning to use a computer

Have students choose one topic. Then write these questions on the board:

1. What did you learn? Who taught you?
2. When did you learn this? Where did you learn this?
3. How did you learn? What steps did you take? What questions did you ask?

Give each student five large (4-inch by 6-inch) index cards or five half-sheets of paper. Have students write their answers to each question on a separate card or paper. Tell students to write complete sentences and that they may need to write more than one sentence for some questions. Model for students how to answer the questions.

Have students volunteer their responses to the questions and write them on the board. Then work with students to draft a personal narrative about the selected topic. Write the draft on the board.

Grammar: Complete and Simple Predicates

PRETEACH Discuss complete predicates and simple predicates with students. Point out the following:

- The **complete predicate** includes all the words that tell what the subject of the sentence is or does.
- The **simple predicate** is the main word or words in the complete predicate.

Write the following sentences on the board and read them aloud:

- *I learned to ride a bike.*
- *I practiced every day.*
- *My uncle helped me.*

Point out the complete and simple predicate in each sentence.

Read the following items aloud. Ask students to identify the complete predicate and the simple predicate in each sentence.

1. First I rode with training wheels. (*rode with training wheels; rode*)
2. Then my uncle took them off. (*took them off; took*)
3. I learned to balance. (*learned to balance; learned*)
4. After that, it was easy. (*was easy; was*)
5. Now I ride my bike to school. (*ride my bike to school; ride*)

> **FLUENCY PRACTICE** Have volunteers read aloud the personal narratives they completed in the writing activity.

Interactive Writing: Personal Narrative

RETEACH Have students try putting the sentences from the Personal Narrative draft in various orders. You may wish to have them conference with partners to help them decide on the best order for the sentences. Once they have done this, encourage them to add more details and to revise the sentences in the draft. Work with students to write a final version of the Personal Narrative. Write it on the board. Then have students copy the revised narrative into their Language Journals.

Grammar-Writing Connection

RETEACH Write these sentences on the board and read them aloud with students: *Mrs. Parks told students that learning is important. "What You Can Learn, What You Can Do" told how learning in school will help students in their jobs.*

Have students work in pairs or in a small group to discuss what jobs they would like to do when they are adults. Then have students draw pictures to show what they will do in their jobs. Encourage students to describe their pictures orally. Then work with them to write a sentence that describes each picture. Review with students complete predicates and simple predicates. Have students label the complete and simple predicates in their sentences. Check students' writing and suggest any corrections they need to make.

FLUENCY PRACTICE Have students choose a favorite paragraph from "What You Can Learn, What You Can Do" to read aloud.

Name _____

A Think about a subject you study in school that you did not read about in "What You Can Learn, What You Can Do." It could be art, music, computers, or another subject. Write the name of the subject on the line.

_____

B Now think of a job you could do using what you learn in that subject. Draw a picture showing a person doing the job.

C Now write a sentence telling about your picture.

_____

_____

TO THE TEACHER Discuss with students careers associated with the subjects they selected in part A above.

Dear Mrs. Parks/What You Can Learn, What You Can Do • **Lesson 4** **25**

© Harcourt

LESSON 5

BEFORE

Building Background and Vocabulary

Build Background/Access Prior Knowledge

Have students look at the illustration on *Pupil Edition* pages 116–117. Tell students that the picture shows a mother and daughter. Their lives changed completely after the girl's father died and a revolution began. Ask students how they think the girl feels about growing up without her father. List students' responses on the board.

Selection Vocabulary

PRETEACH Display Teaching Transparency 46 and read the words aloud. Then point to appropriate parts of the picture as you read the following sentences:

1. This picture is about the Mexican Revolution. Sometimes a **revolution** is a war for freedom.
2. This man is showing **determination**. He does not want to give up.
3. A **ravine** is like a canyon. It is a deep opening in the ground.
4. When the man **plunged** into the ravine, he fell quickly to the ground.
5. The soldiers are pretending to give **condolences**. They are not really trying to comfort the man.
6. In fact, they are **mocking** the man. They are really making fun of him.

AFTER

Building Background and Vocabulary

Selection Vocabulary

RETEACH Revisit Teaching Transparency 46. Read the words with students. Have students work in pairs to discuss the meanings of the words and to answer questions such as: *Does **plunged** mean "fell" or "climbed"?*

Write the following sentence frames on the board. Read each sentence, and ask students to choose a vocabulary word to complete it. Write students' responses in the blanks.

1. It takes _____ to keep trying when you are losing. (*determination*)
2. I jumped off the diving board and _____ into the pool. (*plunged*)
3. Some boys were laughing and _____ us as we played. (*mocking*)
4. I gave my _____ when Hector's grandfather died. (*condolences*)
5. There is a deep _____ behind our school. (*ravine*)
6. The people wanted freedom, so they started a _____. (*revolution*)

Have students write the selection vocabulary words in their Language Dictionaries.

FLUENCY PRACTICE Encourage students to describe the illustration on Teaching Transparency 46 by using the vocabulary words.

Reading "Elena"
pages 116–128

Build Background: "Elena"

Revisit the picture on *Pupil Edition* pages 116–117. Tell students that the woman is Elena and that she is sitting with her daughter. Elena's husband has died. Discuss with students how someone might feel when a parent has died. (*sad, afraid, lonely*)

DISTANT VOYAGES

Focus Skill Narrative Elements

PRETEACH Tell students that every story has a setting, characters, a plot, and a theme. Explain that the setting is when and where the story takes place, and that setting and characters help readers understand the theme. Then draw a chart on the board with the headings *Characters*, *Setting*, and *Theme*. Tell students that this story begins in 1910, at the beginning of the Mexican Revolution. Write this under *Setting*. Once students have read the story, refer back to the chart of narrative elements on the board. Ask students to look through the story again to find information to complete the chart. Help them use details about the characters and the setting to understand the story's theme.

Reading "Elena"

Directed Reading: "Elena"

RETEACH Use these sentences to walk students through the story.

Pages 116–119

- This is Elena, the main character in this story. She is sitting with her daughter.
- This picture shows the day Elena's husband was hurt. He was going to the city on business. His horse plunged into a ravine.
- Elena's husband died three days later. This is Elena. She is very sad.

Pages 120–121

QUESTIONS:
pages 116–121

- Was the girl's father in a car accident? (*no*)
- What is the name of the mother in this story? (*Elena*)
- Where was the girl's father going when he was hurt? (*He was going to the city on business*)

Pages 122–125

- A revolution has started. These soldiers have come to the girl's house. Elena is afraid that the soldiers may rob her or take her son away.
- The soldiers do not harm the family, but Elena decides that they must go away. They take the train to California.

Pages 126–128

- This is Elena with her daughter in their new home in Southern California. The setting has changed from Mexico to California.
- Elena runs a boarding house. She cleans, cooks, and does laundry.

QUESTIONS:
pages 122–128

- Do soldiers come to Elena's house? (*yes*)
- Where do Elena and her family go? (*to California*)
- Why is Elena afraid of the soldiers? (*They may rob her or take her son away.*)

FLUENCY PRACTICE Ask a volunteer to read a paragraph from *Pupil Edition* page 127 aloud. Encourage students to describe the illustration on page 118, and to use as many vocabulary words as they can in their descriptions.

Build Background: "HomeWork"

PRETEACH Remind students that "Elena" is about a girl whose life changes after her father dies. In "HomeWork" they will read about a boy whose father is away. The boy faces some changes, too. Ask students how their lives would change if a parent went away for a time.

English-Language Learners Book

Write the concept words on the board, and use them in sentences to illustrate their meanings.

Concept Words
dishes
kitchen
sink
laundry
cleaning
housework

- Carlos picked up the dirty **dishes**. He took them to the **kitchen**.
- He put the dishes in the **sink** to wash them.
- When his clothes got dirty, he did his own **laundry**.
- Lisa is **cleaning** her room. Carlos and Lisa are doing **housework**.

Have students add these words to their Language Dictionaries.

Directed Reading: "HomeWork"

Summary *Carlos refuses to help with the dishes. A friend told him that such chores are for girls. Carlos learns that his Uncle Rey does housework and cooks. Later Carlos finds out that his father is coming home.*

Use these bulleted sentences to walk students through the story.

Pages 2–3
- Carlos and Lisa are brother and sister. He won't help his sister wash the dishes.
- This is their mother, Mrs. Lopez. She tells Carlos to help.

Pages 4–5
- Carlos says that doing housework is for girls. Carlos's friend Gil told him this.
- Now it is bedtime. Carlos's mother tells Carlos that he can visit Uncle Rey.

Pages 6–11
- Uncle Rey picks up Carlos the next morning.
- Now Carlos is at Uncle Rey's house. Uncle Rey says they should wash the dishes. Carlos is surprised, but he helps anyway.
- Next, Uncle Rey and Carlos do laundry and make hamburgers.

QUESTIONS:
pages 2–11
- Does Carlos help Lisa wash the dishes at home? (*no*)
- Who teaches Carlos to do housework? (*Uncle Rey*)

Pages 12–16
- Back at home, Carlos washes dishes. Lisa and his mother are surprised.
- Carlos also cooks hamburgers. He even does laundry!
- Carlos tells Gil that his uncle cleans and cooks.
- That evening, Carlos's mother tells him that his father is coming home soon.
- Carlos is glad he helped out while his father was away.

QUESTIONS:
pages 12–16
- Has Carlos changed his ideas about housework? (*yes*)
- What does Carlos do after he gets home? (*Responses will vary: washes dishes, cooks hamburgers, does laundry*)

(Focus Skill) Narrative Elements

RETEACH Review setting, characters, plot, and theme with students. Then draw on the board a chart with the headings *Setting*, *Character*, and *Theme*. Ask students to revisit the story and to find details and examples related to the reading. Record students' findings on the chart.

> **FLUENCY PRACTICE** Have students use the illustration on page 12 to retell part of "HomeWork."

Shared Writing: Personal Narrative

PRETEACH Tell students that
they are going to work with you
to write a personal narrative
about a time when a family member or other close person died or

What Happened	How Things Changed
Grandma went to a nursing home.	She wasn't there anymore when I got home from school.
Aunt Maria died.	We don't go to Aunt Maria's for holidays now.

was away for a time. On the board, make a two-column chart like the one
shown. Help students brainstorm sentences about personal experiences to
fill in the chart. Help students phrase their ideas as complete sentences.
Contribute sentences that tell about an experience you have had, so that
you can use these to model writing a paragraph.

Model for students using sentences from the chart to write a narrative
paragraph. Then have students use sentences from the chart to write their
own paragraphs. Tell them that they may make changes to the sentences.

Grammar: Compound Subjects and Predicates

PRETEACH Discuss compound subjects and compound predicates with
students. Point out the following:

- A **compound subject** is two or more subjects that have the same predicate.
- A **compound predicate** is two or more predicates that have the same subject.
- The parts of a compound subject or a compound predicate usually are joined
  by a conjunction such as *and* or *or*.

Write the following sentences on the board, and read them aloud:

- *Gaby and Jorge are in our class.*
- *Their mom got sick and went to the hospital.*
- *Gaby and Jorge visited her or called her every day.*

Tell students that the first sentence has a compound subject (*Gaby*, *Jorge*),
the second has a compound predicate (*got*, *went*), and the third has both
a compound subject and a compound predicate (*Gaby*, *Jorge*; *visited*),
called. Point out the conjunctions *and* and *or* that join the compound
subjects and predicates.

Read the following items aloud. Ask students to say whether each
sentence has a compound subject, a compound predicate, or both.

1. Grandma and Grandpa moved to Florida. (*compound subject*)
2. They call us and send us e-mail. (*compound predicate*)
3. Filiberto and I visit them every summer. (*compound subject*)
4. Still, we miss them and wish they were here. (*compound predicate*)
5. At Christmas they visit us and bring presents. (*compound predicate*)

> **FLUENCY PRACTICE** Have volunteers read aloud the paragraphs they com-
> pleted in the writing activity.

Shared Writing: Personal Narrative

RETEACH Display the paragraph you wrote as a model in the Preteach activity. Read it aloud with students. Ask them what they think needs to be changed and why. Ask students if the paragraph needs more details or if the order of sentences should be changed. Discuss students' suggestions, and incorporate them in a revised version. Then have students revise their own paragraphs, and encourage them to help one another. When students are finished, have them copy their paragraphs into their Language Journals.

Grammar-Writing Connection

RETEACH Write these sentences on the board and read them aloud with students: *Elena's husband died, and her life changed completely. Carlos's father went on a trip, and his life changed in some ways, too.*

Have students work in pairs or in a small group to discuss how it feels when someone close dies or goes away. Then have students draw pictures to show their ideas. Encourage students to describe their pictures orally. Then work with them to write a sentence or two that describes each picture. Ask students to use a compound subject, a compound predicate, or both. Check students' writing and suggest any corrections they need to make.

FLUENCY PRACTICE Have pairs of students choose some dialogue from "HomeWork" to read aloud.

Name _____

A Think of another kind of housework that Carlos could learn to do. Draw a picture showing Carlos doing this chore.

B Write a sentence or two about your picture.

_____

_____

_____

© Harcourt

TO THE TEACHER Work with students to compile
a list of words which describe housework chores.

Elena/HomeWork • **Lesson 5**   **31**

Use with "We'll Never Forget You, Roberto Clemente"

BEFORE

Building Background and Vocabulary

Build Background/Access Prior Knowledge

Discuss with students the concept of teamwork. Ask: **Have you ever been part of a team? What are some good things about being part of a team?** List responses on the board.

Good Things About Teamwork
Team members help one another.
A team can do more than one person alone.
Each member does what he or she is best at.

Selection Vocabulary

PRETEACH Display Teaching Transparency 50, and read the words aloud. Then point to the pictures as you read the following sentences:

1. Workers in the **control tower** help planes take off and land.
2. A light bulb is a source of **artificial** light. A light bulb is a human-made light.
3. This statue is **dedicated** to a baseball player. The statue honors the player.
4. An **ace** player makes even the tough plays. An ace is a great player.
5. Every player makes an **error** now and then. All players make mistakes.
6. Each player plays an important role in the **lineup**. All the players who are on the team are important.

AFTER

Building Background and Vocabulary

Selection Vocabulary

RETEACH Revisit Teaching Transparency 50. Read the words with students. Have students work in pairs to discuss the meanings of the words and to answer questions such as: *Is an* **error** *a good or a bad play?*

Write the following sentence frames on the board. Read each sentence and ask students to choose a vocabulary word to complete it. Write students' responses in the blanks.

1. Does this stadium have grass or _____ turf? (*artificial*)
2. José is not in the _____ today because he is sick. (*lineup*)
3. A worker in the _____ told the pilot to land. (*control tower*)
4. The shortstop made an _____, so I ran to second base. (*error*)
5. Our _____ pitcher is starting today. (*ace*)
6. The new stadium is _____ to all the great players. (*dedicated*)

Have students write the vocabulary words in their Language Dictionaries.

FLUENCY PRACTICE Have students read the completed sentence frames aloud. Encourage them to describe the illustrations on Teaching Transparency 50 using the vocabulary words.

Build Background: "We'll Never Forget You, Roberto Clemente"

PRETEACH Have students look at the pictures on *Pupil Edition* pages 140–141. Tell students that this story is about Roberto Clemente, a talented baseball player. Ask them to share their experiences with baseball. Invite them to tell about their favorite players and teams.

DISTANT VOYAGES

(Focus Skill) Draw Conclusions

PRETEACH Tell students that good readers combine what they already know with information in a story to draw conclusions. Explain that drawing conclusions means figuring out things that the author doesn't tell you. Then draw a chart on the board with the headings *What You Know*, *Information from the Story*, and *Conclusion*. Tell students that you know that the professional baseball season ends each year in October. Write this information in the first column of the chart. Fill in the rest of the chart after students have read the story.

Directed Reading: "We'll Never Forget You, Roberto Clemente"

RETEACH Use these bulleted sentences to walk students through the story.

Pages 140–143

- This is Roberto Clemente, a famous player for the Pittsburgh Pirates.
- This is a baseball card showing Roberto holding his bat, and this card shows him running the bases.
- This fielder is trying to catch a ball that Roberto hit. Will the fielder catch the ball?

Pages 144–145
❓ QUESTIONS: pages 140–145

- Here is Roberto at bat. If he gets a hit, it will be number 3,000.
- Was Roberto Clemente a baseball player? (*yes*)
- What team did Roberto play for? (*Pittsburgh Pirates*)
- In this story, what is he trying to do? (*He is trying to get his 3,000th hit.*)

Pages 146–149

- This is Puerto Rico, where Roberto lived.
- This is Nicaragua. In 1972, there was a big earthquake there.
- Roberto is helping to load a plane that will fly to Nicaragua with supplies.

Pages 150–153

- The plane is taking off. It is evening.
- Roberto is on the plane. People on the ground are waving good-bye to him.
- The plane crashed, and Roberto died.
- Here is what people wrote on a billboard in Pittsburgh. What does it say?

❓ QUESTIONS: pages 146–153

- Did Roberto live in Nicaragua? (*no*)
- What happened in Nicaragua? (*an earthquake*)
- How did Roberto die? (*He died in a plane crash.*)

FLUENCY PRACTICE Ask a volunteer to read a paragraph from *Pupil Edition* page 148 aloud.

BEFORE

Making
Connections
pages 158–159

Concept Words
season
weather
bright
furnace
lights
evening

AFTER

Skill Review
pages 160–161

Build Background: "The Science Fair"

PRETEACH Remind students that "We'll Never Forget You, Roberto Clemente" is about a famous player on a baseball team. In "The Science Fair" they will read about two girls who form a different kind of team. Ask students what school projects they have done with partners or teams.

English
Language
Learners
Book

Write these words on the board, and use them in sentences to illustrate their meanings.
- Summer is the **season** to relax and have fun.
- The **weather** is hot and sunny. The sun is strong and **bright**.
- During the day, the sun can feel like a **furnace**.
- The sunset **lights** up the sky. In the **evening** it is cool and fresh.

Have students add these words to their Language Dictionaries.

Direct Reading: "The Science Fair"

📖 **Summary** *Elena and Kimi work together on a science fair project about the solar system.*

Use these bulleted sentences to walk students through the story.

Pages 2–6
- Elena and Kimi work on a science fair project about the solar system.
- They learn that the sun is 93 million miles away.
- They learn that the sun lights up the moon and why the moon seems to change its shape.
- Elena and Kimi learn that Mercury is the fastest planet in the solar system.

Pages 7–9
- They learn that the weather on Venus is very hot.
- They learn that the Earth's surface actually moves!

❓ **QUESTIONS:**
pages 2–9
- Do Elena and Kimi work together on an art project? (*no*)
- What places have they learned about? (*sun, moon, Mercury, Venus, Earth.*)

Pages 10–13
- Elena and Kimi learn that Mars has craters and volcanoes.
- They learn that the big red spot on Jupiter is a giant storm.
- They learn that Saturn's rings are made of rocks, dust, and ice.

Pages 14–16
- The girls discover that Neptune's moon Triton has a pink ice cap.
- They learn that Pluto's orbit sometimes crosses Neptune's, so that the two planets trade places in the solar system.
- Elena and Kimi create their display. They win first prize!

❓ **QUESTIONS:**
pages 10–16
- Do planets other than Earth have moons? (*yes*)
- What causes the big red spot on Jupiter? (*a storm*)
- What other planets do Elena and Kimi learn about? (*They learn about Mars, Jupiter, Saturn, Uranus, Neptune, and Pluto*)

(Focus Skill) Drawing Conclusions

RETEACH Review the concept of drawing conclusions with students. Then draw on the board a chart like the one you created for the story "We'll Never Forget You, Roberto Clemente." Ask students to revisit "The Science Fair" to complete the chart.

FLUENCY PRACTICE Have students use the illustration on page 5 to retell part of "The Science Fair." Encourage them to use vocabulary words.

Interactive Writing: Paragraph of Information

PRETEACH Tell students that they are going to work with you to write a paragraph of information about the solar system. Ask students to look back at "The Science Fair" and to share what they think are the most interesting facts. Ask them to state the facts in their own words and to use complete sentences. List the sentences on the board.

When you have written five or six sentences, help students develop a topic sentence that states the main idea of the paragraph. Write the topic sentence on the board above the list of sentences. Finally, write all the sentences in paragraph form.

Grammar: Simple and Compound Sentences

PRETEACH Discuss simple and compound sentences with students. Point out the following:

- A **simple sentence** expresses one complete thought.
- A **compound sentence** is two or more simple sentences joined with a conjunction such as *and, or,* or *but* and a comma before the conjunction.

Write the following sentences on the board, and read them aloud:

- *Mercury is close to the sun.*
- *Mercury is close to the sun, and Pluto is far away.*
- *Saturn has rings and moves slowly around the sun.*

Tell students that the first and third sentences are simple sentences, and the second sentence is a compound sentence. Point out that a simple sentence may have a compound subject, a compound predicate, or both. Tell students that the third sentence on the board is a simple sentence with a compound predicate.

Read the following sentences aloud. Ask students to say whether each sentence is a simple sentence or a compound sentence.

1. Jupiter, Saturn, Uranus, and Neptune are called "gas giants." (*simple*)
2. Jupiter has a Great Red Spot, and Neptune has a Great Dark Spot. (*compound*)
3. Neptune is blue, but its moon Triton has pink ice. (*compound*)
4. The days on Mercury are very hot, and the nights are very cold. (*compound*)
5. On Venus, the sun rises in the west! (*compound*)

FLUENCY PRACTICE Have volunteers read aloud the paragraph they completed in the writing activity.

Interactive Writing: Paragraph of Information

RETEACH Display the completed paragraph from the Preteach activity. Read it aloud with students. Ask them if they would make any changes in it and why. Discuss whether the order of sentences needs to be changed or details need to be added. Write the revised paragraph based on students' suggestions. Then have students copy the revised paragraph into their Language Journals. Encourage students to personalize their paragraphs.

Grammar-Writing Connection

RETEACH Write these sentences on the board, and read them aloud with students: *Roberto Clemente was a team player both on the field and off. Elena and Kimi made a winning team for the science fair.*

Have students work in pairs or in a small group to discuss how it feels to be part of a team. Then have students draw pictures to show their ideas. Encourage students to describe their pictures orally. Then work with students to write compound sentences that describe their pictures. Check students' writing and suggest any corrections they need to make.

FLUENCY PRACTICE Have students choose a favorite paragraph or page from "The Science Fair" to read aloud.

Name _____

Do this activity with a partner. Together, think of three science fair projects you could do. Look in your science book for ideas. For each project, write what each teammate would do.

Project Name	What I Will Do	What My Teammate Will Do
_____	_____	_____
_____	_____	_____
_____	_____	_____

© Harcourt

TO THE TEACHER Model for students how to use the table of contents and the index of their science textbooks to find projects.

Use with "Folk Tales from Asia"

Build Background/Access Prior Knowledge

Discuss with students times when they have worked with others. Ask: **What is easy about working together? What is hard?** Record the responses in a chart like the one shown.

Working together is easy because	Working together is hard because
you can share the work.	you have to get along with others.
you get finished faster.	you may not like others' ideas.
you can talk and laugh while you work.	

Selection Vocabulary

PRETEACH Display Teaching Transparency 65, and read the words aloud. Then point to the pictures as you read the following sentences:

1. He **entrusted** the book to the woman. He believed she would take care of it.
2. He **assured** her that it was a good book. He told her that it was definitely good.
3. He **plodded** up the hill. He was walking slowly.
4. It was his **destiny** to climb this hill. He knew that it was his fate.
5. He took notes with **diligence**. He wrote with care and attention.
6. The crop was **bountiful**. They had grown plenty of food.

Selection Vocabulary

RETEACH Revisit Teaching Transparency 65. Read the words with students. Have students work in pairs to discuss the meanings of the words and to answer questions such as: *Does* **plodded** *mean "ran" or "walked"? Does* **bountiful** *mean "a lot" or "a little"?*

Write the following sentence frames on the board. Read each sentence and ask students to choose a vocabulary word to complete it. Write students' responses in the blanks.

1. Sarah's _____ is to be a teacher. (*destiny*)
2. Tomás _____ me that he would help us. (*assured*)
3. Desi _____ home after losing the game. (*plodded*)
4. Gloria _____ her pet parrot to me. (*entrusted*)
5. Esteban worked with _____. (*diligence*)
6. Dad grew a _____ crop of tomatoes. (*bountiful*)

Have students write the selection vocabulary words in their Language Dictionaries.

FLUENCY PRACTICE Have students read the completed sentence frames aloud. Encourage them to describe the illustrations on Teaching Transparency 65 by using the vocabulary words and any other words they know.

Build Background: "Folk Tales from Asia"

DISTANT
VOYAGES

Have students look at the pictures on *Pupil Edition* pages 164–165. Explain that the pictures show the characters from three stories. Tell students that the sun and moon are the main characters in the first story. Explain that in this story the sun and moon are sisters, and things go wrong when the moon tries to be like the sun. Discuss with students what happens when a person tries to be like someone else.

Focus Skill Summarize and Paraphrase

PRETEACH Explain that to summarize a story means to tell main ideas or important events and to paraphrase a story means to retell it in your own words. Explain that when students summarize, they will leave out many details, but when they paraphrase they will include details. Then write on the board *Summary of "How the Moon Became Ivory."* Under this heading write, *Emperor tells the sun to light up the earth during the day.* Continue to summarize and paraphrase main events after students have read the story. Add the information under the heading on the board.

AFTER

Reading "Folk
Tales from Asia"

Pages 166–168

Pages 169–171

Questions:
pages 166–171

Pages 172–175

Pages 176–178

Questions:
pages 172–178

Directed Reading: "Folk Tales from Asia"

RETEACH Use these sentences to walk students through the story.

- This is the sun, and this is the moon. They are sisters.
- When the moon tries to shine as brightly as the sun, the people cannot sleep.
- The moon's face is covered with ashes. Now the moon's light is softer.
- People like the moon's new face.
- Three workers on a farm argue about who is the most important.
- The men get hungry. Panya sees that ants are carrying rice. Then Man finds the rice, and Boon finds their pay.
- The farmer tells the workers that they are all important. They needed one another to find the food and the gold.
- Do the people like the moon's new face? (*yes*)
- What do the men learn from the farmer? (*They learn that they are all important and that they need one another.*)
- This is Virtue. He is telling the foreman that he can work hard.
- The foreman gives Virtue a job as a cook.
- On this day, Virtue did all the work for the whole crew. The other workers are surprised at that.
- The foreman wants to fire everyone but Virtue. Virtue helps them keep their jobs.
- This is Virtue later in his life when he had become a warrior.
- Is Virtue the foreman? (*no*)
- What job does Virtue get? (*cook*)
- What happens to Virtue later in his life? (*He becomes a warrior.*)

FLUENCY PRACTICE Ask students to describe the illustration at the bottom of *Pupil Edition* page 168. Encourage them to use vocabulary words in their descriptions.

Build Background: "Together, We Can Do It"

PRETEACH In "Folk Tales from Asia," students read three stories from different countries. All the stories were about working together. In "Together, We Can Do It," they will read about a crew of workers who painted a big picture on a bridge.

English-
Language
Learners
Book

Write the concept words on the board, and use them in sentences to illustrate their meanings.

Concept Words
connected
countries
workers
crew
finished

- A bridge connects two places. People are **connected**, too.
- People from different **countries** had ideas about the bridge.
- Many **workers** helped clean and paint the bridge.
- The whole **crew** worked on the painting.
- The crew worked on the painting until the painting was **finished**.

Have students add the concept words to their Language Dictionaries.

Directed Reading: "Together, We Can Do It"

Summary *People shared their ideas about what to paint on the Community Bridge. William Cochran used many ideas to paint the bridge. Now the Community Bridge is famous.*

Use these bulleted sentences to walk students through the story.

Pages 2–9
- This is the Community Bridge in Maryland. It had to be painted.
- The workers asked everyone what they should paint on the bridge. They wanted to show the meaning of community.
- First, the bridge had to be cleaned.
- This is William Cochran. He is an artist. The bridge project was his idea.
- Here are things the crew painted on the bridge.

QUESTIONS: pages 2–9
- Did the bridge need to be built? (*no*)
- Where is the bridge? (*in Maryland*)
- What are some things the crew painted on the bridge? (*Responses will vary.*)

Pages 10–16
- Some pictures show the idea of being connected.
- This is a fountain. It looks so real that birds try to drink from it!
- This is a door. It looks real, too.
- This is the bridge after the painting was finished.
- The community had a party when the bridge was finished.

QUESTIONS: pages 10–16
- Does the fountain look real? (*yes*)
- Name one thing that is shown on the bridge? (*Responses will vary.*)
- What did the community do after the bridge was finished? (*They had a party.*)

(Focus Skill) Summarize and Paraphrase

RETEACH Review summarizing and paraphrasing with students. Then write on the board the heading *Summary of "Together, We Can Do It."* Ask students to revisit the story to find main events. List these on the board.

FLUENCY PRACTICE Have students use the illustration on page 15 to retell part of "Together, We Can Do It." Encourage them to use as many vocabulary words and concept words as possible.

Shared Writing: How-To Paragraph

PRETEACH Tell students that they are going to work with you to write a how-to paragraph. Explain that you will write about how to work together to paint a mural. Ask students to think about the supplies and steps involved in painting a group mural. List these ideas on the board as students suggest them.

Ask students to put the steps in the best order, and then help them state each step as a sentence. Finally, write the list of sentences in paragraph form.

1. mural paper
2. paints and brushes
3. pencils or chalk
4. decide what to draw
5. decide what each person will do
6. draw outlines with pencils or chalk
7. paint the mural
8. art smocks

Grammar: Independent and Dependent Clauses

PRETEACH Discuss clauses with students. Point out the following:
- A clause is a group of words that has both a subject and a predicate.
- An **independent clause** can stand alone as a sentence.
- A **dependent clause** cannot stand alone.

Write the following clauses on the board, and read them aloud:
- *Before you begin painting*
- *Draw the picture with chalk*
- *Until the paint dries*

Tell students that the first and third clauses are dependent clauses, and the second clause is an independent clause. Add a period after the independent clause to show that it is a sentence. Add an independent clause after each dependent clause. (*Before you begin painting, draw the picture with chalk. Until the paint dries, leave the mural lying flat.*)

Point out that a comma is used after an introductory dependent clause.

Read the following items aloud. Ask students to say whether each clause is dependent or independent. Then ask them to add an independent clause after each dependent clause to make a sentence. Have students identify the punctuation for each item. (*Possible responses are given.*)
1. If we work together (*dependent; If we work together, we can do it.*)
2. You will need paints and brushes (*independent; You will need paints and brushes.*)
3. We all wear art smocks (*independent; We all wear art smocks.*)
4. Because a mural is a big project (*dependent; Because a mural is a big project, we will not finish it until tomorrow.*)
5. When it is finished (*dependent; When it is finished, we will hang it.*)

FLUENCY PRACTICE Have volunteers read aloud the paragraph they completed in the writing activity.

Shared Writing: How-To Paragraph

RETEACH Display the completed paragraph from the Preteach activity. Read it aloud with students. Ask students if they would make any changes to it and why. Discuss students' suggestions for changes or additions to the paragraph. Write a revised paragraph based on students' suggestions. Then have students copy the revised paragraph into their Language Journals. Encourage students to personalize their paragraphs.

Grammar-Writing Connection

RETEACH Write this sentence on the board, and read it aloud with students: *In "Folk Tales from Asia" and "Together, We Can Do It," we read about people working together.*

Have students work in pairs or in a small group to think of a community project people could work on together. Then have students draw pictures to show their ideas. Encourage students to describe their pictures orally. Then work with them to write a sentence or two that describes each picture. Have students label the clauses in their sentences. Check students' writing and suggest any corrections they need to make.

FLUENCY PRACTICE Have students choose a favorite paragraph or page of "Together, We Can Do It" to read aloud.

Name _____

Make a cover for "Together, We Can Do It." Think of a new title that tells what the story is about. Write your title on your cover. Under the title, draw a picture that shows what the story is about.

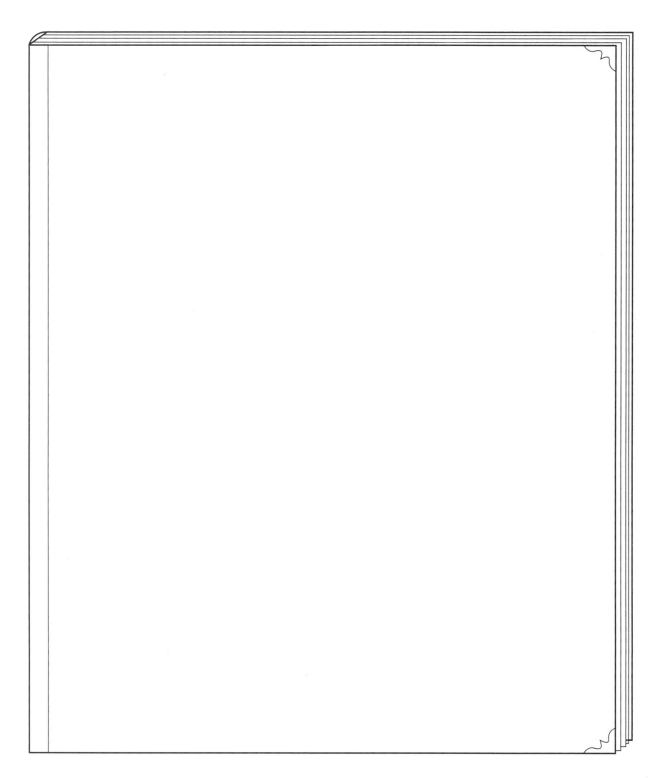

© Harcourt

TO THE TEACHER Model for students the correct capitalization for a story title.

Folk Tales from Asia/Together, We Can Do It • **Lesson 7** **43**

Use with "Iditarod Dream"

Build Background/Access Prior Knowledge

Have students look at the illustrations on *Pupil Edition* pages 186–187. Tell them that the boy and his dogs are in a race across Alaska. The boy and his dogs are working as a team. Ask students to name other kinds of dogs that work with people. (*Possible responses: guide, rescue, police, and show dogs*) Then ask students to share their own experiences with dogs or other animals. Ask: **What things do you do with an animal? What is special about doing things with animals?** Record their responses in a chart like the one shown:

Things I do With Animals	Why These Things Are Special
walk my dog	Dogs love to go for walks.
talk to my bird	My bird can repeat words back to me.
ride my horse	I love to go horseback riding.

Selection Vocabulary

PRETEACH Display Teaching Transparency 75 and read the words aloud. Then point to the pictures as you read the following sentences:

1. This is race **headquarters**. It is the building where the racers must meet before the race starts.
2. These people are **handlers**. They hook the dogs to the sled.
3. The racers are in their starting **positions**. They are in their places.
4. The dogs' lines are in a **tangle**. They are twisted.
5. The racer keeps the dogs at a steady **pace**. He keeps them at the same speed.

Selection Vocabulary

RETEACH Revisit Teaching Transparency 75. Read the words with students. Have students work in pairs to discuss the meanings of the words and to answer questions such as: *Is a **headquarters** a mountain or a building*? *Do **handlers** take care of dogs or sleds*?

Write the following sentence frames on the board. Read each frame and ask students to choose a vocabulary word to complete it. Write students' responses in the blanks.

1. The _____ help with the dogs. (*handlers*)
2. The lead dog sets the _____ that others must beat. (*pace*)
3. The race begins near the _____. (*headquarters*)
4. At race time, the racers take their _____. (*positions*)
5. Racers hope their lines do not get in a _____. (*tangle*)

Have students write the selection vocabulary words in their Language Dictionaries.

FLUENCY PRACTICE Encourage students to describe the illustrations on Teaching Transparency 75 by using the vocabulary words.

Build Background: "Iditarod Dream"

Revisit the pictures on *Pupil Edition* pages 186–187. Tell students that the boy is named Dusty. He and his dogs are in the Jr. Iditarod race in Alaska. Dusty and his dogs are a team. Ask: **What do you think it would feel like to be in a sled-dog race?**

DISTANT VOYAGES

 Draw Conclusions

PRETEACH Tell students that good readers combine what they already know with information in a story to draw conclusions. Explain that drawing conclusions means figuring out things that the author doesn't tell you. Then draw a chart on the board with the headings *Prior Knowledge*, *Information from the Story*, and *Conclusion*. Explain that you know that a good starting position in a race is an advantage. Write this information under *Prior Knowledge*. After students have read the story, ask them to look through the story to find details to complete the chart. (*The story says that there are fifteen racers and that Dusty starts sixth.*) Ask students what conclusion they can draw about Dusty's starting position. (*Dusty has a good starting position.*)

AFTER

Reading
"Iditarod Dream"

Pages 186–189

Pages 190–191

❓ QUESTIONS:
pages 186–191

Pages 192–193

Pages 194–196

❓ QUESTIONS:
pages 192–196

Directed Reading: "Iditarod Dream"

RETEACH Use these sentences to walk students through the story.

- These dogs are pulling a sled in a race. The boy you see is steering the sled.
- The boy with the red hood and green jacket is Dusty. He is a racer.
- Dusty is hugging one of his sled dogs.
- This picture shows the sled packed with supplies.
- Dusty's team is ready to start. The team's number is 6.
- Dusty's dogs are huskies. The harness and the lines connect the dogs to one another and to the sled.
- Is Dusty going to be in the race? (*yes*)
- What number is Dusty's team? (*6*)
- What conclusions can you draw about the team's starting position in the race? (*It is in a good position.*)
- What will Dusty be doing during the race? (*He will be driving the sled.*)
- This is a moose. Dusty hopes he won't see one because moose sometimes attack dogs.
- It is Dusty and his team will spend the night at the halfway point in the race station.
- Dusty puts ointment, or cream, on his dogs' feet.
- Dusty melts snow so the dogs can drink.
- Here is Dusty winning first place. Reporters are taking his picture.
- Does Dusty see a moose during the race? (*no*)
- What does Dusty put on his dogs' feet? (*ointment or cream*)
- What happens at the end of the race? (*Dusty wins the race. Reporters take his picture.*)

FLUENCY PRACTICE Ask students to use vocabulary words to describe the illustration on *Pupil Edition* page 190.

Build Background: "Race the Wind"

PRETEACH Remind students that "Iditarod Dream" is about a boy and his dogs who win a dog-sled race. In "Race the Wind" students will learn more about traveling by dogsled. Ask students if they would like to travel by dogsled.

English-
Language
Learners
Book

Concept Words
gloves
hat
mittens
hood
boots
scarf

Write the concept words on the board. Use them in sentences to illustrate their meanings.

- I wear **gloves** to keep my hands warm and a **hat** to keep my head warm.
- My little sister wears **mittens** on her hands.
- There is a **hood** on the back of my jacket to keep my head covered.
- **Boots** keep my feet warm and dry.
- I wrap a **scarf** around my neck to keep it warm.

Have students add the concept words to their Language Dictionaries.

AFTER

Skill Review
pages 200–201

Directed Reading: "Race the Wind"

📖 **Summary** *People who drive dogsleds are called mushers. The most famous sled-dog race is the Iditarod. The Junior Iditarod is an event for younger mushers.*

Use these sentences to walk students through the story.

Pages 2–5
- Dogs are pulling the sled over the snow.
- The man is guiding the dogs.
- Sled dogs sometimes wear boots to protect their feet.
- Mushers wear gloves, hats, and scarves to keep themselves warm.

Pages 6–9
- Mushers sometimes wear snowshoes on their feet.
- This sled is ready to go.

❓ QUESTIONS:
pages 2–9
- Who pulls the sled? (*the sled dogs*)
- What do the sled dogs sometimes wear to protect their feet? (*boots*)
- Why do mushers wear scarves and gloves? (*to keep themselves warm.*)

Pages 10–11
- Here is a family at the Junior Iditarod.
- Look at the young musher; he is getting his sled ready for a race.

Pages 12–13
- This musher is packing his sled.

Pages 14–16
- Mushers carry food, water, clothes, and other supplies.
- People have come from all over the world to race dogsleds.
- The dogs look strong, healthy, and ready to race.
- The crowd cheers as a dogsled team races by.

❓ QUESTIONS:
pages 10–16
- In what competition do young mushers race? (*Junior Iditarod*)
- Why do mushers train hard? (*Mushers train hard in order to win the race.*)

⭐(Focus Skill) Draw Conclusions

RETEACH Review the concept of drawing conclusions with students. Then draw a chart on the board with the headings *Prior Knowledge*, *Information from the Story*, and *Conclusion*. Ask students to revisit the story to find information to complete the chart. record students' findings on the chart.

FLUENCY PRACTICE Ask students to read a favorite paragraph or page of "Race the Wind."

Interactive Writing: Summary

PRETEACH Tell students that they are going to work with you to write a summary of "Race the Wind." Remind students that a summary tells the important events or main ideas in a story. Ask students to recall main ideas from the story and list them on the board.

Ask students if any main ideas are missing and if the ideas are in the correct order. Then ask students to state each main idea as a sentence, and write the sentences on the board in list form. Finally, write the sentences as a summary in paragraph form.

1. People in the Far North travel by dogsled.

2. Samoyeds, huskies, and malamutes are strong and have thick fur.

3. Mushers are dogsled drivers.

Grammar: Complex Sentence

PRETEACH Point out the following to students:
- A complex sentence contains an independent clause and at least one dependent clause.
- A dependent clause often begins with a connecting word, such as *before, after, because*, or *if*.

Write the following sentences on the board, and read them aloud:
- *Mushers wear warm clothes because it is very cold.*
- *After they race, mushers and dogs need to rest.*
- *Mushers wear boots.*

Tell students that the first two sentences are complex sentences, the third one is a simple sentence. Show students the dependent and independent clauses in the sentences. In the first sentence, *mushers wear warm clothes* is the independent clause; *because it is very cold* is the dependent clause. In the second sentence, *After they race* is the dependent clause; *mushers and dogs need to rest* is the independent clause.

Point out that a dependent clause at the beginning of a sentence is usually followed by a comma; a dependent clause at the end of a sentence usually does not have a comma before it.

Read the following items aloud. Ask students to say whether each sentence is a complex sentence or not.
1. Mushers and their dogs work as a team. (*no*)
2. Mushers wear snowshoes when they walk in deep snow. (*yes*)
3. Because they have thick fur, the dogs stay warm. (*yes*)
4. The dogs are a team. (*no*)
5. The musher must stop if the dogs' lines get tangled. (*yes*)

FLUENCY PRACTICE Have volunteers read aloud the summary they completed in the writing activity.

Interactive Writing: Summary

RETEACH   Display the completed summary from the Preteach activity. Read it aloud with students. Ask them what changes they would like to make. Discuss students' suggestions for changes or additions to the summary. Write the revised summary based on students' suggestions. Then have students copy the summary into their Language Journals. Encourage students to personalize their summaries.

Grammar-Writing Connection

RETEACH   Write these sentences on the board, and read them aloud with students:

"Iditarod Dream" is about a boy who won a sled-dog race. "Race the Wind" tells more about how a musher and his or her dogs work together as a team.

Have students work in pairs or in a small group to discuss ways in which people and animals work or play together as a team. Then have students draw pictures to show their ideas. Encourage students to describe their pictures orally. Then work with them to write a complex sentence that describes each picture. Remind students that a complex sentence has an independent clause and at least one dependent clause. Check students' writing and suggest any corrections they need to make.

FLUENCY PRACTICE   Have students use the illustration on pages 10–11 to retell part of "Race the Wind." Encourage them to use as many vocabulary words and concept words as possible.

Name _____

Look at the diagram on pages 8–9 of "Race the Wind." Then think about how you travel and what you wear. Draw a diagram like the one in the story. Instead of a dogsled, show what you travel in or on. Show what you wear when you travel. Write labels to identify the items you drew.

© Harcourt

TO THE TEACHER Model for students how to connect a label with an illustration.

Iditarod Dream/Race the Wind • **Lesson 8** **49**

Use with **"Woodsong"**

Build Background/Access Prior Knowledge

Have students look at the illustration on *Pupil Edition* page 205. Explain that it is a picture of a sled dog that belonged to the man who wrote the story. Ask students what they remember about sled dogs from "Iditarod Dream." Encourage them to share their own experiences with dogs. Ask: **How do you feel about your dog or a dog you know? Why do you feel this way?** Record students' responses in a chart like the one shown:

How I feel About My Dog	Why I Feel This Way
I love my dog.	I have had my dog since he was a puppy.
I miss him when I am not home.	I always like being with my dog.

Selection Vocabulary

PRETEACH Display Teaching Transparency 84 and read the words aloud. Then point to the pictures as you read the following sentences:

1. The dogs **snort** in the cold air. They breathe out of their noses forcefully.
2. She **resembled** her sister in the picture. She looked like her sister.
3. The **bulk** of the box made it hard to move. It was large and heavy.
4. You **disengage** the brake before driving. You release the brake.
5. She told him **pointedly** she was unhappy. She made herself very clear.
6. The horse wears a **harness** so he can pull the plow.
7. He has **retired** from his job. He does not go to work anymore.

Selection Vocabulary

RETEACH Revisit Teaching Transparency 84. Read the words with students. Have students work in pairs to discuss the meanings of the words and to answer questions such as: *If you resembled your mother, would you look like her?*

Write the following sentence frames on the board. Read each frame and ask students to choose a vocabulary word to complete it. Write students' responses in the blanks.

1. The dogs bark and _____ when they play. (*snort*)
2. The oldest dog _____ from pulling the sled. (*retired*)
3. The two smallest dogs _____ each other. (*resembled*)
4. The sweater under my coat added _____ to my size. (*bulk*)
5. The sled will move when you _____ the brake. (*disengage*)
6. A _____ connects the dogs to the sled. (*harness*)
7. _____ he told us to be quiet. (*Pointedly*)

Have students write the selection vocabulary words in their Language Dictionaries.

FLUENCY PRACTICE Have students read the sentence frames aloud.

BEFORE

Reading
"Woodsong"
pages 204–214

Build Background: "Woodsong"

Revisit the picture on *Pupil Edition* page 205. Tell students that this sled dog is named Storm. Explain that Storm was a special dog who belonged to the author of the story. Tell students that they will read about the friendship between Storm and his owner. Explain that sometimes Storm used a stick to communicate with his owner. Discuss with students ways in which dogs communicate with people. (*barking, tail wagging, growling, jumping*)

DISTANT VOYAGES

 ## Summarize and Paraphrase

PRETEACH Tell students that to summarize means to tell the most important ideas of a story using the author's words and their own words. Explain that to paraphrase means to retell the story in their own words. Then make two charts on the board, one for summarizing (*Author's Words, Your Own Words*, and *Summary*), and one for paraphrasing (*Author's Words, Paraphrase*). In both charts, next to *Author's Words*, write *At peak, he was a mighty dog. He pulled like a machine.* Work with students to complete the charts after students have read the story.

AFTER

Reading
"Woodsong"

Directed Reading: "Woodsong"

RETEACH Use these sentences to walk students through the story.

Pages 204–207

- This is a sled dog named Storm. He has a stick.
- This is what a dog-sled team might look like from above.
- Storm is one of the dogs on the team.

Pages 208–209

- The author found his hat under some snow.
- Storm buried the hat as a joke. The author says that when he found his hat, Storm smiled.

 QUESTIONS:
pages 204–209

- What is the sled dog named? (*Storm*)
- What did Storm bury under the snow? (*a hat*)
- What does the author say Storm did when the author found his hat? (*The author says Storm smiled.*)

Pages 210–211

- A very heavy stove is on the sled.
- All the dogs are sleeping except Storm.

Pages 212–214

- Storm has a stick in his mouth. When something is wrong, Storm drops it. This is how Storm tells his owner that he is making the dogs work too hard.

QUESTIONS:
pages 210–214

- Was Storm a smart dog? (*yes*)
- What made the sled heavy? (*a stove*)
- What did it mean when Storm dropped the stick? (*It meant that something was wrong.*)

FLUENCY PRACTICE Encourage students to describe the illustration on *Pupil Edition* pages 210–211. Suggest they use vocabulary words in their descriptions.

Build Background: "Good Dog!"

PRETEACH Remind students that "Woodsong" is about a dog who communicated with his owner using a stick. In "Good Dog!" students will read about how to teach dogs to do different things.

English-Language Learners Book

Write the concept words on the board. Use them in sentences to illustrate their meanings.

Concept Words
rules
special
together
leash
fetch
wags

- There are **rules** to follow when you train a dog.
- Dogs love to get **special** treats.
- People and dogs do many things **together**.
- My dog is always on a **leash** when I take him for a walk.
- If you throw a ball, some dogs will **fetch** it.
- A happy dog **wags** its tail.

Have students add the concept words to their Language Dictionaries.

Directed Reading: "Good Dog!"

Summary *For people and dogs to live together happily, people must tell their dogs what they want them to do. Dogs can be trained to heel, sit, stay, lie down, jump up, come, shake hands and fetch.*

Use these sentences to walk students through the story.

Pages 2–5
- Here is a dog with his owner. They both look very happy.
- This family wants to buy a dog. One puppy really likes them.
- This dog was naughty. He made a big mess.
- Here is a boy playing with his dog in the snow.

Pages 6–7
- This must be a good dog. He is getting a treat.
- Here are two girls running with their dog.

QUESTIONS: pages 2–7
- Who can be friends with dogs? (*people*)
- What are the two girls doing with their dog? (*running*)
- How do people reward good dogs? (*People often give them treats.*)

Pages 8–9
- This girl is teaching her dog to heel. He is learning to stay right beside her.
- These people are teaching their dogs to sit.

Pages 10–13
- This dog is learning to stay. He is learning not to move until he is told.
- By saying "Up!" this girl got her dog to jump onto her lap.
- This boy told his dog to come. The dog is coming to him.

Pages 14–16
- This dog has been taught how to shake with his paw.
- This dog is playing fetch. He ran after a stick and is bringing it to his owner.

QUESTIONS: pages 8–16
- Does "Heel" mean "lie down" or "stay close"? (*stay close*)
- What game do most dogs love to play? (*fetch*)
- What should a dog do after it catches a stick? (*The dog should bring the stick back to the person who threw it.*)

★ Focus Skill) Summarize and Paraphrase

RETEACH Review summarizing and paraphrasing with students. Then write on the board a chart with the headings *Author's Words* and *Paraphrase*. Ask students to revisit the story and to choose a paragraph to paraphrase. Record a volunteers paraphrased paragraph and the corresponding author's paragraph on the chart.

FLUENCY PRACTICE Ask students to read aloud a favorite paragraph or page from "Good Dog!"

Interactive Writing: How-To Paragraph

PRETEACH Tell students that they are going to work with you to write a how-to paragraph using time order. Tell them that they will write a paragraph about how to give a dog a bath. Ask students why they think time order would be the best way to arrange the paragraph. Generate a concept web with the phrase *How to Give a Dog a Bath* in the center circle. In the surrounding circles, write: *get the dog wet, put shampoo on the dog, wash the dog, rinse the dog.* Brainstorm with students additional steps to add to the web.

Ask for volunteers to come to the board and write the steps listed in the web in time order.

Write the displayed sentence frames on the board. Using the time-ordered steps students generated, ask them to fill in the blanks.

How to Give a Dog a Bath

When you give a dog a bath, the first thing you need to do is _____ . Then you _____ . Next, you _____ . The last thing you do when you give a dog a bath is _____ .

Grammar: Common and Proper Nouns

PRETEACH Discuss common and proper nouns with students. Point out the following:

- A noun names a person, a place, a thing, or an idea.
- A common noun names any person, place, thing, or idea and begins with a lowercase letter.
- A proper noun is the name or title of a specific person, place, or thing. Each important word of a proper noun begins with a capital letter.

Write the following sentences on the board and read them aloud:

- *Sara has a dog named Blue.*
- *Blue had puppies in February.*
- *The Montoyas got a puppy and named him Cactus.*

Point out the common nouns and proper nouns in these sentences. In the first sentence, *dog* is a common noun; *Sara* and *Blue* are proper nouns. In the second sentence, *puppies* is a common noun; *Blue* and *February* are proper nouns. In the last sentence, *puppy* is a common noun; *Montoyas* and *Cactus* are proper nouns.

Read the following items aloud. Ask students to say whether each noun is a common noun or a proper noun.

1. Monday (*proper*)   2. Chicago (*proper*)   3. city (*common*)
4. month (*common*)   5. Pedro (*proper*)

FLUENCY PRACTICE Have volunteers read aloud the paragraph they completed in the writing activity.

Interactive Writing: How-To Paragraph

RETEACH Display the completed paragraph from the Preteach activity. Read it aloud with students. Ask them what revisions they would like to make to it. Discuss students' suggestions for changes or additions to the paragraph. Ask students if there are any additional steps they wish to include. Write the revised paragraph based on students' suggestions. Then have students copy the paragraph into their Language Journals. Encourage students to personalize their paragraphs.

Grammar-Writing Connection

RETEACH Write these sentences on the board, and read them aloud with students:

"Woodsong" is about a dog named Storm and the things Storm taught his owner. "Good Dog" is about how to train your dog so the two of you can be a team.

Have students work in pairs or in a small group to discuss things that dogs and people teach each other. Then have students draw pictures to show their ideas. Encourage students to describe their pictures orally. Then work with them to write a sentence or two that describes each picture. Have students label the common nouns and proper nouns in their sentences. Check students' writing and suggest any corrections they need to make.

FLUENCY PRACTICE Have students use the illustration on page 10 to retell part of "Good Dog!" Encourage students to use as many vocabulary words and concept words as possible.

Name _____

Reread the paragraph you wrote about how to give a dog a bath.
Now draw pictures that show the steps in your paragraph. Write a caption for each step. A caption describes what is shown in a picture.

© Harcourt

TO THE TEACHER Model for students how to capitalize the words in a caption.

LESSON 10

Use with "Island of the Blue Dolphins"

BEFORE
Building Background and Vocabulary

Build Background/Access Prior Knowledge

Discuss with students times when they helped someone who needed help. Ask: **Have you ever helped someone in an emergency? What did you do? How did it make you feel to help the person?** Record students' responses on the board.

Selection Vocabulary

PRETEACH Display Teaching Transparency 94 and read the words aloud. Then point to the pictures as you read the following sentences:

1. The foxes are resting in their **lair**.
2. This **abalone** has a pretty shell.
3. Pat had a stomachache after he **gorged** himself with so much food.
4. This girl is **vainer** than her friends. She is always looking in the mirror.
5. The boat **pitched** wildly on the big waves. It rocked up and down and from side to side.
6. The boy standing by himself looks lost and **forlorn**.
7. Marsha was **overcome** with joy when she heard that her favorite cousin was coming to visit her.

AFTER
Building Background and Vocabulary

Selection Vocabulary

RETEACH Revisit Teaching Transparency 94. Read the words with students. Have students work in pairs to discuss the meanings of the words and to answer questions such as: *If you are **forlorn**, are you happy or sad? Is an **abalone** a bird or a shellfish?*

Write the following sentence frames on the board. Read each frame, and ask students to choose a vocabulary word to complete it. Write students' responses in the blanks.

1. Juan was _____ with fear when he looked down from the cliff. (*overcome*)
2. We _____ ourselves with pizza and then felt sick. (*gorged*)
3. Carmen found the shell of an _____ on the beach. (*abalone*)
4. The little boat _____ on the stormy sea. (*pitched*)
5. Both girls are pretty, but Ana is _____ than Maria. (*vainer*)
6. The coyotes are resting in their _____. (*lair*)
7. The lost boy looked sad and _____. (*forlorn*)

Have students write the selection vocabulary words in their Language Dictionaries.

FLUENCY PRACTICE Have students read the completed sentence frames aloud. Encourage them to describe the illustrations on Teaching Transparency 94 by using the vocabulary words and any other words they know.

**Reading
"Island of the Blue
Dolphins"**
pages 226–236

Build Background: "Island of the Blue Dolphins"

Tell students that "Island of the Blue Dolphins" is about Ramo and his sister Karana. Explain to them that when the people of the island have to leave it, they all get on a ship. When Karana gets on, she cannot find her brother on the ship. Have students predict what Karana will do. Ask: **What do you think Karana will do when she finds out that her brother is not on the ship? Why do you think she will do this? What would you do?**

DISTANT VOYAGES

⭐ (Focus Skill) Narrative Elements

PRETEACH Tell students that a story includes narrative elements—characters, setting, plot, and theme. Explain that characters are the people, animals, or things the story is about. The setting is when and where the story takes place, and the plot is what happens in the story. The theme is the message of the story. Then draw a chart on the board with the headings *Setting*, *Characters*, *Plot*, and *Theme*. Tell students that this story takes place on an island off the coast of California a long time ago. Enter this information under *Setting*. After students have read the story, ask them to revisit it to find details to complete the chart. Record students' findings.

**Reading
"Island of the Blue
Dolphins"**

Pages 226–229

Pages 230–231

🔍 QUESTIONS:
pages 226–231

Pages 232–233

Pages 234–236

🔍 QUESTIONS:
pages 232–236

Directed Reading: "Island of the Blue Dolphins"

RETEACH Use these sentences to walk students through the story.
- This is the island where Karana lives. The island is the setting of the story, and Karana is the main character.
- This ship will take Karana and her people to a new home.
- The people are hurrying to the boats.
- The boats will take the people out to the ship, which is anchored outside the cove.
- Karana is on the ship. The storm is getting worse.
- Karana is worried. She cannot find her brother on the ship.
- Karana sees Ramo, on the island. He has been left behind.
- Who is Ramo? (*Karana's brother*)
- Why are the people leaving the island? (*to go to a new home*)
- Why is Karana worried? (*She cannot find her brother on the ship.*)
- Karana dives into the sea. She is swimming back to the island.
- At first, Karena holds a basket with her things in it, then she lets it go.
- It is night on the island. Karana and Ramo are sitting by a fire.
- Two days go by. Karana and Ramo look for ships, but they do not see any.
- Karana and Ramo discuss what they will do to survive on the island.
- How does Karana get back to the island where Ramo is? (*she swims*)
- What are Karana and Ramo looking for? (*ships*)
- What do Karana and Ramo talk about at the end of the story? (*They talk about what they will do on the island alone.*)

FLUENCY PRACTICE Encourage students to describe the illustration on *Pupil Edition* pages 230–231 by using vocabulary words in their descriptions.

Build Background: "Wave Rider"

PRETEACH Remind students that "Island of the Blue Dolphins" is about Karana, who swims back to the island to help her brother. Tell students that in "Wave Rider" they will read about Roy who, even though he is afraid, helps his friend.

Write the concept words on the board. Use them in sentences to illustrate their meanings.

Concept Words
beach
afraid
waves
swimmer
swam
dive

- We go to the **beach** every summer.
- Eduardo is **afraid** to try surfing. He thinks the **waves** are too high.
- Dina is a good **swimmer**. She **swam** out to the boat.
- She also learned to **dive** off the pier.

Have students add the concept words to their Language Dictionaries.

Directed Reading: "Wave Rider"

📖 **Summary** *Roy is an good swimmer, but he is afraid of the ocean. He overcomes his fear in a dream. At the beach, his friend Luis slips and falls into the water. Roy overcomes his fear of the ocean to save his friend.*

Use these sentences to walk students through the story.

Pages 2–5
- The boys are having fun at the beach.
- Jimmy and Luis are playing in the waves. Roy is on the beach.
- Now the boys are at the pool.
- Roy is diving into the deep end of the pool. He is a good swimmer.

Pages 6–9
- The boys race across the pool. Roy is winning, and Jimmy is second.
- Now the boys are in bed.
- Roy wishes he were not afraid to swim in the ocean.
- In Roy's dream, he is riding a wave and having fun.
- Roy wakes up. He is not afraid of the waves anymore.

❓ QUESTIONS: pages 2–9
- What kind of a swimmer is Roy? (*a good one*)
- What is Roy afraid of? (*the ocean; waves*)
- What does Roy wish for? (*He wishes that he were not afraid of the ocean.*)

Pages 10–16
- The boys are getting ready to go to the beach. Luis takes a paper bag to collect shells.
- The boys are climbing the sand dunes.
- Luis is collecting shells by the rocks. Roy and Jimmy are playing catch.
- Luis slips on the rocks and falls into the ocean. Luis needs help.
- Roy is afraid, but he dives in and swims to help his friend Luis.
- Roy and Luis are riding a wave back to the beach. Roy has saved Luis.

❓ QUESTIONS: pages 10–16
- Is it a windy or a calm day? (*It is windy.*)
- What does Luis take to the beach with him? (*a paper bag*)
- Why does Roy dive in the ocean? (*Roy dives in the ocean to save Luis.*)

⭐(Focus Skill) Narrative Elements

RETEACH Review narrative elements with students. Then draw a chart on the board with the headings *Setting*, *Characters*, *Plot*, and *Theme*. Ask students to revisit the story to find details to complete the chart. Record students' findings on the chart.

> **FLUENCY PRACTICE** Ask students to read aloud a favorite paragraph or page of "Wave Rider."

Interactive Writing: Paragraph That Explains

PRETEACH Tell students that they are going to write a paragraph that explains. Tell them that many subjects, such as history, science, and math, rely on writing that explains. Tell students that their topic will be why students have fire drills. Generate a concept web with the phrase *Why We Have Fire Drills* in the center circle. Help students brainstorm phrases related to the topic to add to the web.

Help students state each phrase as a sentence, and write the sentences on the board. Work with students to arrange the sentences in a logical order. Finally, use the sentences to write a draft of the paragraph.

Grammar: Singular and Plural Nouns

PRETEACH Discuss singular and plural nouns with students. Point out the following:

- A singular noun names one person, place, thing, or idea.
- A plural noun names more than one person, place, thing, or idea.
- Regular nouns become plural when you add *s* or *es*.

Write the following sentences on the board and read them aloud:

- *We saw two boats at the beach.*
- *There are many beaches in Florida.*
- *Flies were buzzing around the boat.*

Point out the singular nouns and the plural nouns in the sentences. In the first sentence, *boat* is plural, *beach* is singular. In the second sentence, *beaches* is plural, *Florida* is singular. In the third sentence, *flies* is plural, *boat* is singular.

Call students' attention to the *s* and *es* endings of the plural nouns, *boats*, *beaches*, and *flies*. Tell students that *flies* is the plural of *fly* and that when a noun ends with a consonant followed by *y*, the *y* changes to *i* before *es* is added.

Read the following items aloud. Ask students to say whether each noun is singular or plural. Ask students to say the plural form of each singular noun and the singular form of each plural noun.

1. waves (*plural; wave*)   2. swimmer (*singular; swimmers*)
3. friend (*singular; friends*)   4. lunches (*plural; lunch*)
5. guppy (*singular; guppies*)

FLUENCY PRACTICE Have volunteers read aloud the paragraph they completed in the writing activity.

Interactive Writing: Paragraph That Explains

RETEACH Display the draft version of the paragraph from the Preteach activity. Read it aloud with students. Ask them what changes they would like to make to it. Discuss students' suggestions for changes or additions to the paragraph. Write the revised paragraph based on students' suggestions. Then have students copy the revised paragraph into their Language Journals. Encourage students to personalize their paragraphs.

Grammar-Writing Connection

RETEACH Write these sentences on the board, and read them aloud with students: *In "Island of the Blue Dolphins," Karana helped her brother. In "Wave Rider," Roy helped his friend.*

Have students work in pairs or in small groups to discuss different ways to help others. Then have students draw pictures to show their ideas. Encourage students to describe their pictures orally. Then work with them to write a sentence or two that describes each picture. Have students label the singular and plural nouns in their sentences. Check students' writing and suggest any corrections they need to make.

FLUENCY PRACTICE Then, have students use the illustration on page 8 to retell part of "Wave Rider." Encourage students to use as many vocabulary words and concept words as possible.

Name _____

A Draw a picture of a beach.
Add people, animals, boats, or other things to make your picture interesting.

┌───┐
│   │
│   │
│   │
│   │
│   │
│   │
│   │
│   │
│   │
│   │
│   │
│   │
│   │
│   │
└───┘

B Make your beach the setting for a story.
Write a sentence that describes your beach setting.

_____

_____

_____

TO THE TEACHER Model for students examples of story setting
sentences. Make sure to include phrases that describe where
and when.

Island of the Blue Dolphins/Wave Rider • **Lesson 10**   **61**

© Harcourt

Use with "Everglades"

BEFORE

Building Background and Vocabulary

Build Background/Access Prior Knowledge

Have students look at the illustrations on *Pupil Edition* pages 248–249. Tell students that this is the Everglades, a very special river. It is always changing. Ask students to share their experiences about places that have changed over time. Ask: **Do you know of a place that has changed? How has it changed?** Record their responses in a chart like the one shown.

Place	How It Has Changed
the creek that runs through the park	It has almost dried up, because it hasn't rained.
the empty lot down the street	A shoe store is being built there.
our school	We moved into a new school building this year.

Selection Vocabulary

PRETEACH Display Teaching Transparency 104, and read the words aloud. Then point to the pictures as you read the following sentences:

1. The sailors **pondered** the future. They thought carefully about what might happen to them.
2. For **eons** people have sailed. They have been sailing for a long time.
3. A **multitude** of dolphins live in the sea. Many of them live there.
4. The sailor **scurried** up the net. He moved quickly to the top.
5. Florida is a **peninsula**. It has water on all sides except one.
6. There is more than enough to eat because there is a **plenitude** of food.

AFTER

Building Background and Vocabulary

Selection Vocabulary

RETEACH Revisit Teaching Transparency 104. Read the words aloud with students. Have students work in pairs to discuss the meanings of the words and to answer questions such as: *Does **multitude** mean "very many" or "very few"?*

Write the following sentence frames on the board. Read each one aloud and ask students to choose a vocabulary word to complete it. Write students' responses in the blanks.

1. The stars have been shining in the sky for _____. (*eons*)
2. Roberto _____ the huge size of the ocean. (*pondered*)
3. On the ocean, you can see a _____ of stars. (*multitude*)
4. A squirrel _____ quickly up the tree. (*scurried*)
5. The river provides a _____ of fresh water. (*plenitude*)
6. A _____ is almost an island. (*peninsula*)

Have students write the selection vocabulary words in their Language Dictionaries.

FLUENCY PRACTICE Encourage students to describe the illustrations on Teaching Transparency 104 by using the vocabulary words and any other words they know.

Build Background: "Everglades"

Have students look at the illustration on *Pupil Edition* page 251. Tell students that the man is a storyteller and is telling the children about the river, known as the Everglades. He is telling them how the river has changed over time. Ask students how they think the river might have changed.

DISTANT VOYAGES

 Prefixes, Suffixes, and Roots

PRETEACH Tell students that they can use what they know about prefixes, suffixes, and root words to help them figure out the meanings of new words. On the board, begin a two-column chart of words made up of these word parts. Begin the chart by writing *root + root* in the first column and *pesti (pest) + cides (killers) = pesticides (pest killers)* in the second column. Point out that *pesticides* is formed by combining the two roots. After students have read the story, direct them to look through it again to find examples of other words that have been formed by combining word parts.

AFTER
Reading
"Everglades"

Pages 248–253

Pages 254–257

❓ QUESTIONS:
pages 248–257

Pages 258–261

Pages 262–267

❓ QUESTIONS:
pages 258–267

Directed Reading: "Everglades"

RETEACH Use these sentences to walk students through the story.

- Five children are in a boat. The storyteller is telling them about the river.
- This river is called the Everglades. It is in Florida.
- The river is very wide and shallow.
- The boat is a pole boat. The man is pushing it with a pole.
- This picture shows how the river began eons ago.

- This is saw grass. The man says that the grass is very sharp.
- Multitudes of birds, alligators, and other animals lived near the river.

- Are the children in a sailboat? (*no*)
- Where is the Everglades? (*Florida*)
- What animals lived there? (*Animals that lived there include birds, alligators, and turtles. Accept all reasonable responses.*)

- This is a panther. Panthers, raccoons, and other animals lived here, too.
- This man is a Native American. He is a Seminole Indian.
- This is an egret. The man explains that hunters killed most of the egrets.

- This beautiful flower is an orchid. Unfortunately, people picked all the orchids.
- Other types of birds died or were killed, too.
- Farms and towns were built. Then many more animals died.
- The children are sad when they hear the man's story.
- The man tells them that they can make changes to protect the Everglades.

- Did Native Americans live near the Everglades? (*yes*)
- Who killed the egrets and alligators? (*hunters*)
- Why are the children sad? (*Responses will vary; most of the animals and some of the plants have died.*)

FLUENCY PRACTICE Ask a volunteer to read aloud a paragraph from *Pupil Edition* page 254.

Build Background: "Dear Grandma"

PRETEACH Remind students that "Everglades" is about a river in Florida and how it has changed. In "Dear Grandma" students will read about a boy named Tomás who is going through a big change at a new school.

English-
Language
Learners
Book

Write the concept words on the board. Use them in sentences to illustrate their meanings.

Concept Words
sign
song
time
brave
miss

- The street **sign** says "Stop."
- I heard a new **song** on the radio.
- George Washington lived a long **time** ago.
- A **brave** girl saved a cat from the river.
- I **miss** many things about El Salvador.

Have students add the concept words to their Language Dictionaries.

Directed Reading "Dear Grandma"

📖 **Summary** *Tomás writes letters to his grandmother about what he learns in his new school. In time, Tomás learns to like the changes in his new place.*

Use these sentences to walk students through the story.

Pages 2–5
- This is a letter that Tomás wrote to his grandmother. He misses her.
- Tomás is learning "The Star-Spangled Banner."
- This is Fabiola, Tomás's friend. They are reading their part of the song.

Pages 6–9
- Mrs. Clark, the school librarian, helps Tomás learn about Benjamin Franklin.
- The teacher says this boy is like Rip Van Winkle because he is yawning.
- Tomás learns that Rip, a character in a story, sleeps for a long time.

❓ **QUESTIONS:**
pages 2–9
- Does the school librarian help Tomás? (*yes*)
- To whom does Tomás write letters? (*his grandmother*)

Pages 10–13
- Fabiola tells Tomás who Johnny Appleseed is.
- At the school library Tomás learns about a brave woman named Rosa Parks and a baseball player named Jackie Robinson.

Pages 14–16
- Tomás learned all the words of "The Star-Spangled Banner." He wrote them down for his grandmother.
- Tomás's grandmother sent him a sign that says "Yes, I can!"

❓ **QUESTIONS:**
pages 10–16
- What did Tomás's grandmother send him? (*a sign*)
- What did Tomás do after he learned all the words to "The Star-Spangled Banner"? (*He wrote them down for his grandmother.*)

★ Focus Skill Prefixes, Suffixes, and Roots

RETEACH Review prefixes, suffixes, and root words with students. Then write on the board a two-column chart with *prefix + root word* in the first column and *ex (to bring out) + plain (clear) = explain (to bring out the meaning clearly).* in the second column. Ask students to revisit the story to find examples of words formed of combining a prefix and a root word. Add the examples to the chart.

FLUENCY PRACTICE Ask students to read all or part of their favorite letter from the story "Dear Grandma."

Interactive Writing: Friendly Letter

PRETEACH Tell students that they are going to work with you to write a letter to someone they know. In their letters, students will write about how a place has changed. Brainstorm with students a place to write about. After you choose a place, write a chart on the board like the one shown, and help students brainstorm words and phrases to fill in the first column.

Have students use the words and phrases from the first column to make sentences for the second column. Write the sentences the students suggest.

How It Was Before	How It Is Now
empty lot	It is a garden.
full of broken glass and trash	Glass and trash are gone.
covered with weeds	Flowers and vegetables are growing.

Have each student use the sentences to write his or her own friendly letter to someone he or she knows. Model the parts and body of a friendly letter by writing one of your own on the board.

Grammar: Possessive Nouns

PRETEACH Review possessive nouns with students. Point out the following:

- A **possessive noun** shows ownership.
- To form the possessives of most singular nouns, add 's.
- To form the possessives of plural nouns ending in s, add only an apostrophe.
- To form the possessives of plural nouns that do not end in s, add 's.

Write the following sentences on the board, and read them aloud:

- *The bird's nest is in the tree.*
- *The frogs' chirps sound like music.*
- *The children's lunches are ready.*

Tell students that *bird's* is a possessive singular noun; *frogs'* is a possessive plural noun; and *children's* is the possessive form of a plural noun that does not end in *s*. Point out what was added to each noun to form the possessive.

Write the following words on the board. Ask students to say whether each possessive noun is singular or plural.

1. the turtle's tail (*singular*)
2. the river's fish (*singular*)
3. the men's boat (*plural*)
4. the seagulls' calls (*plural*)
5. the boys' mother (plural)

> **FLUENCY PRACTICE** Have volunteers read aloud the letters they completed in the writing activity.

Interactive Writing: Friendly Letter

RETEACH Display the model letter from the Preteach activity. Read it aloud with students. Ask students what changes they would make to it. Discuss students' suggestions for changes or additions to the letter. Write a revised letter based on students' suggestions. Then have students revise their own letters. Encourage them to talk with one another about their revisions. Have students copy their revised letters into their Language Journals.

Grammar-Writing Connection

RETEACH Write these sentences on the board, and read them aloud with students:

- *In "Everglades," things changed. They got worse.*
- *In "Dear Grandma," things changed. They got better for Tomás.*
- *For me, things changed. They got _____.*

Have students work in pairs or in small groups to discuss things that have changed for the better or for the worse in their own lives. Have students write two or three sentences. They should use the sentence frame from the board as the first sentence about how things have changed. Ask students to use possessive nouns in their sentences. Check students' writing and suggest any corrections they need to make. Then have students draw pictures to show their ideas. Encourage students to describe their pictures orally.

FLUENCY PRACTICE Have students use the illustrations on pages 8–9 to retell part of "Dear Grandma".

Name _____

A Sentences 1–6 tell how a frog's egg changes to become a frog. Draw pictures to show what the sentences tell.

1. This is a frog's egg. It is in a river.	**2.** The egg becomes a tiny tadpole. It lives in the river.	**3.** The tadpole gets bigger. It grows legs in back.
4. The tadpole gets bigger and grows little legs in front. Its tail gets smaller.	**5.** The tadpole's legs are bigger, and its tail is almost gone.	**6.** The tail is gone. The frog can swim, but it has to live on land now.

B What do you think the frog might say about the big change it made? Write your answer in a sentence or two.

_____

_____

TO THE TEACHER Explain to students what a tadpole is. Provide students with a book that illustrates and describes the development of a tadpole into a frog.

© Harcourt

LESSON 12

Use with **"Summer of Fire"**

BEFORE
Building Background and Vocabulary

Build Background/Access Prior Knowledge

Give students drawing materials, and have them draw a picture of a fire. Encourage students to share and talk about their drawings. Ask students to discuss what they know about fire. Ask: **What are some good things about fire? What are some bad things?** Record the responses in a chart like this one.

Good Things	Bad Things
Fire can help keep you warm.	Fire can hurt people and animals.
You can cook food over a fire.	Fire can burn down buildings.
Campfires are fun.	Fires can get out of control.

Selection Vocabulary

PRETEACH Display Teaching Transparency 114, and read the words aloud. Then point to the pictures as you read the following sentences:

1. As the sun went down, the light **dwindled**.
2. Do not feed the wild animals. That is a good **policy**.
3. A **geyser** shoots hot water high into the air.
4. This tent has a **canopy** on it for shade.
5. The road **veered** here. It turned away from the main road.
6. Dry leaves and sticks make good **tinder** to start a fire.
7. This campfire has burned down to **embers**. Now it is just hot coals.

AFTER
Building Background and Vocabulary

Selection Vocabulary

RETEACH Revisit Teaching Transparency 114. Read the words aloud with students. Have students work in pairs to discuss the meanings of the words and to answer questions such as: *Is a* **canopy** *a covering or a chair? If daylight has* **dwindled**, *is it brighter or darker outside?*

Write the following sentence frames on the board. Read each one aloud, and ask students to choose a vocabulary word to complete it. Write students' responses in the blanks.

1. The park's _____ does not allow campfires. (*policy*)
2. A few hot _____ can start a big fire. (*embers*)
3. People love to see the _____ named Old Faithful. (*geyser*)
4. The number of campers _____ when it rained. (*dwindled*)
5. The path _____ toward the river. (*veered*)
6. We needed _____ to start our fire. (*tinder*)
7. It was shady under the _____ of trees. (*canopy*)

Have students write the selection words in their Language Dictionaries.

FLUENCY PRACTICE Have students read the sentence frames aloud. Encourage them to describe the illustrations on Teaching Transparency 114 by using the vocabulary words and any other words they know.

Build Background: "Summer of Fire"

Have students look at the pictures on *Pupil Edition* pages 276–277. Tell them that this is a forest fire. Ask students to discuss what they know about forest fires. How do they start? What can get burned? How are the fires put out?

DISTANT VOYAGES

(Focus Skill) Graphic Aids

PRETEACH Tell students that maps, charts, diagrams, and graphs are different kinds of **graphic aids**. Explain that graphic aids show information from a selection. Write the title *Ways Fires Were Started in Yellowstone* on the board. Ask students to look through the story to find the two ways fires were started in the summer of 1988. (*lightning, cigarette*) Write the responses under the title. Then ask students to draw pictures next to each way the fires were started. Help students label their pictures. Tell students that this graphic aid, will help readers better understand what started the fires. After students have read the story, help them create another graphic aid of their choosing using information from the selection.

 AFTER

Reading
"Summer of Fire"

Pages 276–281

🔎 QUESTIONS:
pages 276–281

Directed Reading: "Summer of Fire"

RETEACH Use these sentences to walk students through the story.

- The forest is on fire. The fire is red and yellow.
- The fire is making a lot of smoke. It is hard to see the animals.
- If lightning strikes a tree, it can start a fire. Often, rain puts out these fires.
- In the summer of 1988, lightning started many fires in Yellowstone National Park. This map a graphic aid. It shows where the fires burned that summer.

- Were the fires in the story caused by animals? (*no*)
- What often puts out forest fires? (*rain*)
- What does the map show? (*The map shows the location of forest fires in Yellowstone in the summer of 1988.*)

Pages 282–286

- Fire fighters tried to put out the fires, but they could only help put out the small ones.
- The fires spread through the forest very fast.
- Some fires burned until it snowed that winter.
- Too much fire is bad, but it is a part of nature. Fire helps the forest begin again.

🔎 QUESTIONS:
pages 282–286

- Is fire always bad for the forest? (*no*)
- What finally put out all the fires? (*snow*)
- Why were the fire fighters unable to put out the fires? (*They spread too fast.*)

FLUENCY PRACTICE Have students describe the illustration on *Pupil Edition* pages 276–277. Encourage them to use as many vocabulary words as they can in their descriptions.

Build Background: "Ring of Fire"

PRETEACH Remind students that "Summer of Fire" is about the fires in Yellowstone in 1988. In "Ring of Fire," students will learn more about what happens during and after a forest fire. Ask students what they think happens after a forest fire.

English-
Language
Learners
Book

Write concept words on the board. Use them in sentences to illustrate their meanings.

Concept Words
smoke
sparks
heat
burned
bark

- The **smoke** from the fire made it hard to see.
- Bright **sparks** flew from the fire.
- The sun and fire are two sources of **heat**.
- The fire **burned** many trees and plants.
- The trunk of a tree is covered with **bark**.

Have students add the concept words to their Language Dictionaries.

Directed Reading: "Ring of Fire"

Summary *Lightning can spark a forest fire, but it is mostly people who start one. Shortly after the fire, a healthy forest begins to grow.*

Use these sentences to walk students through the story.

Pages 2–5
- It has not rained here for two months. Look at the dry leaves and twigs.
- Lightning hits a tree in the forest. Sparks fly, and the dry forest catches fire.
- Deer and other animals run away from the fire.
- This graph shows that people cause most forest fires.

Pages 6–9
- This is a forest after a fire. Almost everything has burned.
- Old evergreen trees have very thick bark. It protects the trees from fire.
- These pinecones have been opened by the heat of the fire. Their seeds will fall on the ground and grow into new trees.

QUESTIONS: pages 2–9
- According to the graph, does lightning cause most forest fires? (*no*)
- What protects old evergreens from fire? (*their bark*)
- What does fire do to pinecones? (*It causes their seeds to fall out and grow.*)

Pages 10–13
- Burned leaves and twigs get the forests soil ready for plants.
- These fire fighters are trying to put out a fire.
- This time line shows what happens after a forest fire. After three years, the forest is again covered with green plants.

Pages 14–16
- These elk are eating grass and wildflowers. This is a young forest.
- Look at this strong, healthy forest. It grew out of a forest fire.

QUESTIONS: pages 10–16
- Do grass and wildflowers grow in a young forest? (*yes*)
- How do burned leaves help the forest? (*They get the soil ready to feed old and new plants.*)

(Focus Skill) Graphic Aids

RETEACH Review the concept of and types of graphic aids with students. Then draw on the board a one-column chart with the heading *Good Things About Forest Fires*. Ask students to revisit the story to find information to complete the chart.

FLUENCY PRACTICE Have students use the graph on page 13 to retell part of "Ring of Fire."

Shared Writing: Persuasive Paragraph

PRETEACH Explain that persuasive writing convinces readers to do or not to do something. Tell students that they are going to work with you to write persuasive paragraphs and that the audience for their paragraphs will be younger children. The topic will be *Don't play with matches.* Generate a concept web with the topic in the center. Brainstorm with students reasons why children should not play with matches, and fill in the web.

you could hurt yourself

Don't play with matches

other people could get hurt

your home could catch fire

Write the following topic sentence on the board, and suggest students use it to begin their paragraphs: *Children should not play with matches because _____.* Work with students to state each reason from the concept web as a sentence. Write the sentences on the board.

Have students work independently to organize the sentences into paragraphs. Provide students with a model by writing your own paragraph on the board.

Grammar: Pronouns and Antecedents

PRETEACH Discuss pronouns and antecedents with students. Point out the following:

- A **pronoun** is a word that takes the place of one or more nouns.
- The **antecedent** of a pronoun is the noun or nouns to which the pronoun refers.
- Pronouns show **number** and **gender**. Number tells whether the pronoun is singular or plural. Gender tells whether the pronoun is masculine, feminine, or neuter. Pronouns agree in number and gender with their antecedents.

Write the following sentences on the board, and read them aloud:

1. Maria and Josie like to sing. They wrote a song.
2. My brother went camping, and he saw a raccoon.
3. Linda heard thunder. Then she saw lightning.

Point out the pronoun and its antecedent in each sentence.

1. *They; Maria; Josie*   2. *he; brother*   3. *she; Linda*
1. *plural, feminine*   2. *singular; masculine*   3. *singular, feminine*

Call students' attention to the number and gender of each pronoun.

Write the following items on the board, and read them aloud. Ask students to name each pronoun and its antecedent.

1. Police must be strong. They also must be brave. (*They; police*)
2. My dad went on a trip, but he is back now. (*he; dad*)
3. My book got wet, and it is ruined. (*it; book*)

FLUENCY PRACTICE Have volunteers read aloud the paragraphs they completed in the writing activity.

Interactive Writing: Persuasive Paragraph

RETEACH Display the model paragraph from the Preteach activity. Read it aloud with students. Ask students what changes need to be made. Discuss students' suggestions for changes or additions to the paragraph. Write a revised paragraph based on students' suggestions. Then have students revise their own paragraphs and copy the revised paragraphs into their Language Journals.

Grammar-Writing Connection

RETEACH Write these sentences on the board, and read them aloud with students:

Fire fighters are hard workers. They risk their lives to keep other people and animals safe.

Ask students to identify the pronoun in the sentences. (*They*). Write the following pronouns on the board: *he, she, it, they, you, we, I*. Have students work in pairs to write a short paragraph about what they know about fire fighters. Ask them to use at least three of the pronouns from the board in their sentences. Tell students that the sentences from the board should be the first two sentences in their paragraph.

Ask for volunteers to read the completed paragraph to the class. Check students' writing for the correct use of pronouns, and suggest any corrections they need to make.

FLUENCY PRACTICE Have students choose a favorite paragraph or page of "Ring of Fire" to read aloud.

Name _____

Reread the paragraph you wrote on the topic *Don't play with matches.* Use this space to create a poster on the same topic. Draw a picture that will persuade children not to play with matches. Also write some of the reasons and examples from your paragraph. Make your poster as persuasive as you can.

© Harcourt

TO THE TEACHER Before students begin drawing their posters, review their paragraphs on the topic. Make sure they have included persuasive examples and reasons which they can illustrate.

LESSON 13

Use with "Oceans"

BEFORE

Building Background and Vocabulary

Build Background/Access Prior Knowledge

Have students look at the illustrations on *Pupil Edition* pages 298–299. Tell students that this is an ocean. Point out the wave. Encourage students to discuss their knowledge about the ocean. Draw a five-senses organizer on the board. Ask students to tell what they might see, hear, smell, taste, and touch at the ocean. Record students' responses on the organizer.

sights: waves boats

tastes: salt

At the ocean

touch

sounds

smells

Selection Vocabulary

PRETEACH Display Teaching Transparency 123, and read the words aloud. Then point to the pictures as you read the following sentences.

1. The moon's gravity pulls water up from the Earth's surface. This is called **gravitational** pull.
2. High tide, or a **bulge**, happens when the Earth's ocean waters are pulled outward.
3. The sun is a source of **energy**. Energy is power.
4. At low tide, the water is **shallow**. It is not deep.
5. The boat sailed into the **inlet**. The little bay was a safe place to anchor.
6. Electricity is **generated** at power plants. Power plants make electricity.

AFTER

Building Background and Vocabulary

Selection Vocabulary

RETEACH Revisit Teaching Transparency 123. Read the words aloud with students. Have students work in pairs to discuss the meanings of the words and to answer questions such as: *Does* **shallow** *mean "deep" or "not deep"?*

Write the following sentence frames on the board. Read each one aloud, and ask students to choose a vocabulary word to complete it. Write students' responses in the blanks.

1. Power plants can make _____ from moving water. (*energy*)
2. Power can be _____ from many different sources. (*generated*)
3. We like to wade in _____ water. (*shallow*)
4. _____ pull causes the Earth's tides. (*Gravitational*)
5. The _____ is a good place to swim because the water is calm. (*inlet*)
6. A _____, or high tide, occurs as the Earth rotates. (*bulge*)

Have students write these words in their Language Dictionaries.

FLUENCY PRACTICE Have students read the completed sentence frames aloud.

74   Lesson 13 • *English-Language Learners Teacher's Guide*

Build Background: "Oceans"

Revisit the pictures on *Pupil Edition* pages 298–299. Point out the big wave on the ocean. Ask students how they imagine it would feel to be in a boat sailing on the waves.

DISTANT
VOYAGES

(Focus Skill) Main Idea and Details

PRETEACH Tell students that the pattern of main idea and details is one way to organize information in a selection like "Oceans." Remind students that the main idea is what a topic is mostly about. Point out that the author divides the selection into three topics: Tides, Tsunamis, and Waves. Tell students that each topic has a main idea. Have students select one of the topics and write its name on the board. Then draw an organizer like the one shown. Model how to complete the chart by filling in one detail box with topic-related information from the selection. Help students complete the remaining detail boxes and main idea box after they have read the story.

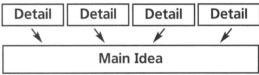

Detail	Detail	Detail	Detail
Main Idea			

Directed Reading: "Oceans"

RETEACH Use these sentences to walk students through the story.

Pages 298–301
- Look at the ocean. Here is a big wave.
- This is the Earth. It is the only planet with liquid water on the surface.
- These diagrams tell about tides. Tides happen because gravitational pull causes ocean water to rise and fall.

Pages 302–303
- These pictures show low tide and high tide at the same place on the beach.
- The main topic of this part of the selection is waves. The writer gives many details about waves.
- Look at the three pictures that shows a tsunami hitting land in Hawaii.

QUESTIONS: pages 298–303
- Is Earth the only planet with liquid water on the surface? (*yes*)
- What causes ocean water to rise and fall? (*gravitational pull*)
- What is happening in the the pictures of the tsunami? (*Responses will vary.*)

Pages 304–307
- Big and little waves are made by wind blowing the water.
- The wind moves the waves in all different directions.
- This diagram shows the energy in waves.

Pages 308–310
- These waves coming to shore are called breakers.
- The waves on this Hawaiian beach break slowly on the shore.
- Waves are powerful. Over a long period of time, they even wear away rocks.

QUESTIONS: pages 304–310
- Can waves wear away rocks? (*yes*)
- What are waves called when they come to shore? (*breakers*)
- What causes waves? (*wind blowing the water*)

FLUENCY PRACTICE Encourage students to describe the illustration on *Pupil Edition* page 302 by using as many vocabulary words as they can in their descriptions.

Build Background: "Sea Gifts"

PRETEACH Remind students that "Oceans" tells about tides and waves. In "Sea Gifts" students will read about many good things that come from the sea. Ask students to name some things that from the sea. (*Responses will vary.*)

English-
Language
Learners
Book

Concept Words
clouds
oil
natural resources
power plant
transportation

Write the concept words on the board. Use them in sentences to illustrate their meanings.

- Rain falls from **clouds** in the sky.
- We get **oil** and gas from under the Earth's surface.
- One of the **natural resources** that comes from the sea is salt.
- A **power plant** is a factory that makes energy.
- Cars, bikes, and boats are all forms of **transportation**.

Have students add these words to their Language Dictionaries.

Directed Reading: "Sea Gifts"

Summary *The sea gives the Earth many gifts. These gifts include water, food, natural resources, and transportation.*

Use these sentences to walk students through the story.

Pages 2–5
- The main idea of this selection is that the sea gives us many gifts.
- The globe shows that oceans cover more than half of the Earth.
- A cow is drinking water. Water is the most important sea gift.
- This diagram shows what happens to water from the sea.

Pages 6–9
- People eat sea animals such as fish, shrimp, and lobster.
- Salt is a natural resource. When seawater dries up sea salt is left.
- Oil, another natural resource, comes out of rocks under the sea.

QUESTIONS: pages 2–9
- Is water the most important sea gift? (*yes*)
- What is one kind of food we get from the sea? (*Responses may vary; fish.*)
- How do we get sea salt? (*When seawater dries up sea salt is left.*)

Pages: 10–16
- This page is about how people use the sea to travel.
- The people at the beach are having fun and keeping the sea clean.
- Sharks, squid, and other tropical fish live in the sea.

QUESTIONS: pages 10–16
- Do sharks live in the sea? (*yes*)
- What is inside the oyster? (*a pearl*)
- What are some of the gifts we get from the sea? (*Responses will vary; water, food, salt, oil, transportation, fun*)

(Focus Skill) Main Idea and Details

RETEACH Review the concept of main idea and details with students. Then draw on the board an organizer like the one on *Teacher's Guide* page 75. Ask students to select one of the topics from the selection and record its main idea and details on the organizer. Model how to complete the organizer by filling in one detail box. Suggest students revisit the story to find information to complete the organizer.

FLUENCY PRACTICE Ask students to read a paragraph or a page from the selection that tells about their favorite sea gift.

Interactive Writing: Persuasive Letter

PRETEACH Tell students that they are going to work with you to write a persuasive letter to the editor of a local newspaper. Their audience will be the newspaper's readers. Explain that persuasive writing convinces readers to do something. The topic will be *Keep the beach and ocean clean* or another topic of your choice. Generate a chart like the one shown.

Brainstorm with students a list of reasons and actions to support the topic. Write them in the chart.

Work with students to develop an opinion sentence. For example: *People should keep the beach clean because trash left behind may harm animals.* Then have them state the supporting reasons and the actions from the chart as sentences.

Keep the beach and ocean clean	
Reasons	**Actions**
Trash may harm sea animals.	Do not throw trash in the water.
Trash ruins the beauty of the beach.	Take your trash home or put it in trashcans.

Finally have students work in pairs to organize the sentences into a letter to the editor.

Model the form and content of a persuasive letter by writing a draft of your own letter on the board. Encourage students to refer to it as they write their letters.

Grammar: Subject and Object Pronouns

PRETEACH Discuss subject and object pronouns with students. Point out the following:

- A **subject pronoun** takes the place of a noun or nouns in the subject of a sentence. Subject pronouns are *I, you, he, she, it, we,* and *they.*
- An **object pronoun** takes the place of a noun after an action verb or a preposition. Object pronouns are *me, you, him, her, it, us,* and *them.*

Write the following sentences on the board, and read them aloud:
1. *I gave him my book.* 2. *She is calling you.*
3. *We eat lunch with them.*

Point out the subject pronoun and the object pronoun in each sentence.

1. *I, him* 2. *She, you*
3. *We, them)*

Write these sentences on the board, and read them aloud. Ask students to name the pronoun in each sentence and to say whether it is a subject or an object pronoun.

1. I sent Ana a letter. (*I; subject pronoun*)
2. Ana answered it. (*it; object pronoun*)
3. The teacher gave us a test. (*us; object pronoun*)
4. You can call Jorge back. (*you; subject pronoun*)

FLUENCY PRACTICE Have volunteers read aloud the letters they completed in the writing activity.

Interactive Writing: Persuasive Letter

RETEACH Display the draft of the letter you wrote from the Preteach activity. Read it aloud with students. Ask them what they think you need to change and why. Ask: **Have I stated my opinion clearly? Have I given persuasive reasons and examples? Have I asked for specific action?** Discuss students' suggestions for changes or additions to the letter. Write a revised letter based on students' suggestions. Then have students revise their own letters and copy the revised letters into their Language Journals.

Grammar-Writing Connection

RETEACH Have students work in pairs or in a small group to discuss what they have learned about oceans or gifts from the sea. Then have students draw pictures to show something that they have learned. Encourage students to describe their pictures orally. Then work with students to write a sentence or two that describes each picture. Encourage students to use pronouns in their sentences and to label the subject and object pronouns. Check students' writing and suggest any corrections they need to make.

FLUENCY PRACTICE Have students use the illustrations on pages 8–9 retell part of "Sea Gifts."

You can use the organizer below to show the main idea and details of "Sea Gifts."
Write one important detail in each of the four smaller boxes. If you want, look back at
the story to find important details. Then write the main idea of the story in the big
box at the bottom.

Detail	Detail	Detail	Detail

Main Idea

© Harcourt

TO THE TEACHER If students are having difficulty with the
task, suggest that they select one topic or one gift from the
sea that is described in the selection. Work with students to
identify the topic sentence and supporting details.

Use with **"Seeing Earth from Space"**

Build Background/Access Prior Knowledge

Show students a globe. Ask them to imagine that they are astronauts looking down at Earth. Tell them to think about what they might see. **Would the Earth look healthy and beautiful, or would it look sick? Would you see clean, blue oceans or pollution or both?** Give students paper and crayons or markers, and ask them to draw pictures of what Earth might look like from space. Encourage students to share their pictures.

Selection Vocabulary

PRETEACH Display Teaching Transparency 133, and read the words aloud. Then point to the pictures as you read the following sentences:

1. The moon is **barren**. There is no life on the moon.
2. This spacecraft has **sensors** that collect information.
3. Most rivers do not flow in a straight line. They curve and **meander**.
4. An **atoll** is a ring-shaped island.
5. The water in the middle of the atoll is called a **lagoon**.
6. A **reef** is a strip of sand or coral just beneath the surface of the water.

Selection Vocabulary

RETEACH Revisit Teaching Transparency 133. Read aloud the words with students. Have students work in pairs to discuss the meanings of the words and to answer questions such as: *Does* **barren** *mean "full of life" or "lifeless"? If a road* **meanders**, *is it curved or straight?*

Write the following sentence frames on the board. Read each sentence aloud, and ask students to choose a vocabulary word to complete it. Write students' responses in the blanks.

1. Some boats have _____ that tell how deep the water is. (*sensors*)
2. Many fish live on this coral _____ (*reef*)
3. The water in the _____ is warm. (*lagoon*)
4. Walk straight to the boat; don't _____. (*meander*)
5. The _____ looks like a floating circle. (*atoll*)
6. This island is _____ because very little rain falls here. (*barren*)

Have students write the selection vocabulary words in their Language Dictionaries.

> **FLUENCY PRACTICE** Have students read the completed sentence frames aloud. Encourage them to describe the illustrations on Teaching Transparency 133 by using the vocabulary words and any other words they know.

Build Background: "Seeing Earth from Space"

Have students look at the pictures on *Pupil Edition* pages 324–325. Tell students that astronauts in space took these pictures of Earth. Ask: **If you were an astronaut, what part of Earth would you take a picture of?**

DISTANT VOYAGES

Graphic Aids

PRETEACH Remind students that graphic aids help readers "see" and understand information. Explain that a **diagram** is a graphic aid that shows the parts of something. A diagram can also show how a process happens. Then draw on the board a diagram showing the parts of an atoll. Tell students that in "Seeing Earth from Space" they will learn how an atoll forms. After students read the story, help them add information to the diagram to show how an atoll forms.

Directed Reading: "Seeing Earth from Space"

RETEACH Use these sentences to walk students through the story.

Pages 322–327
- These photographs show different parts of Earth as seen from space.
- Astronauts took these pictures on their way to the moon.
- This is a photo of a big storm called Typhoon Pat.
- This is what air pollution over the Indian Ocean looks like from space.

Pages 328–331
- Here is an island. It was created when a volcano erupted beneath the ocean.
- This is the island of Hawaii. It was created by volcanoes, too.
- The volcanoes that made these islands are sinking. There will be lagoons in the middle instead of land. The ring-shaped islands will be atolls.

QUESTIONS: pages 322–331
- Can air pollution be seen from space? (*yes*)
- What created Hawaii? (*volcanoes*)
- How is an atoll formed? (*Responses will vary; a volcano sinks.*)

Pages 332–335
- These islands have already become atolls.
- These are the Himalaya Mountains in Asia.
- If you were standing on the moon, this is what the Earth would look like!

Pages 336–338
- Soil flows into the sea if all the trees are cut down.
- This is Earth's atmosphere. The red part is the air we breathe.
- This is sand from the Sahara in Africa. It is blowing toward the Americas. This shows that it's a small world, and we all must take care of it.

QUESTIONS: pages 332–338
- Are the Himalaya Mountains in the Americas? (*no*)
- Where is the Sahara? (*Africa*)
- Why do we all need to work together to take care of the Earth? (*Responses will vary—because it's a small world, what happens in one place affects other places far away.*)

FLUENCY PRACTICE Ask volunteers to describe the photographs on *Pupil Edition* pages 330–331. Encourage them to use vocabulary words in their descriptions.

Build Background: "Kids Care"

PRETEACH Remind students that "Seeing Earth from Space" shows photographs of Earth taken from space and tells what we learn from these pictures. In "Kids Care" students will read about things children do to take care of the Earth.

English-
Language
Learners
Book

Write the concept words on the board. Use them in sentences to illustrate their meanings.

Concept Words
pollution
litter
waste
leaky
faucet

- Smoke is one kind of air **pollution**.
- Broken glass and other **litter** can harm animals.
- Don't **waste** water. Try to save water instead.
- A **leaky faucet** drips water down the drain.

Have students add these words to their Language Dictionaries.

Directed Reading: "Kids Care"

Summary *In this selection, kids show that they care about the Earth. Picking up litter, saving water, recycling, riding bikes, and planting trees are some things kids can do to help the Earth.*

Use these sentences to walk students through the story.

Pages 2–5
- One park is clean and beautiful, but another is full of litter.
- A child is throwing trash in a trash can. This kid cares about the Earth.
- These students are working together. They are putting litter into trash bags.

Pages 6–9
- We use water for drinking, growing food, cooking food, and washing clothes.
- Look at the leaky faucet. A lot of water is being wasted.
- One way to save water is to fill the tub only half full.

**QUESTIONS:
pages 2–9**
- Do we use water for growing food? (*yes*)
- What is another word for trash? (*litter*)
- What are some ways we can save water? (*Responses will vary—fix leaky faucets; turn off water when brushing teeth; fill the bathtub only half full.*)

Pages 10–13
- Look at the big pile of trash. We can take care of the Earth by recycling trash.
- Paper comes from trees. When we recycle paper, we save trees.
- This chart shows things we can recycle.
- Smoke from factories and gases from cars can pollute the air.

Pages 14–16
- These children are growing vegetables.
- These children are planting trees. This is a good way to help the Earth.

**QUESTIONS:
pages 10–16**
- Does planting trees help the Earth? (*yes*)
- Where does paper come from? (*trees*)
- Name a thing you can do to take care of the Earth. (*Responses will vary.*)

(Focus Skill) Graphic Aids

RETEACH Remind students that one type of graphic aid is a chart. Have them revisit the story, and help them make a chart on the board showing all the things kids can do to help the Earth.

FLUENCY PRACTICE Ask students to read aloud a favorite paragraph or page of "Kids Care."

Interactive Writing: Persuasive Announcement

PRETEACH Tell students that they are going to work with you to write persuasive announcements. Explain that persuasive writing convinces readers to do something or not to do something. Tell students that their announcements should persuade other students to join a recycling campaign. Generate a chart like the one shown. Brainstorm with students what information and persuasive reasons to include in their announcements.

Join Our Recycling Campaign	
Information	**Reasons**
What we will recycle: newspaper cardboard cans glass	save trees and other resources
Where to bring things to recycle: Outside school library	save space in landfills

Work with students to develop a headline for their announcements and to state reasons as sentences. Write the sentences on the board.

Have students work independently to organize the information and reasons into announcements. Encourage students to add drawings to make their announcements more persuasive. Model this form of writing by writing a draft of your own announcement on the board.

Grammar: Possessive Pronouns

PRETEACH Discuss possessive pronouns with students. Point out the following:

- A **possessive pronoun** shows ownership. It takes the place of a possessive noun.
- One kind of possessive pronoun is used before a noun. These pronouns are *my, your, his, her, its, our,* and *their.*
- The other kind of possessive pronoun stands alone. These pronouns are *mine, yours, his, hers, ours,* and *theirs.*

Write the following sentences on the board, and read them aloud:

- *The Earth is my home, and it is also your home.*
- *The Earth is mine, and it is also yours.*

Point out that in the first sentence the pronouns *my* and *your* are used before nouns and that in the second sentence the pronouns *mine* and *yours* stand alone.

Read the following sentences aloud. Ask students to identify the possessive pronoun in each one and to say whether it is used before a noun or stands alone.

1. The recycling project was his idea. (*his; before a noun*)
2. The Villarosas recycle their newspapers. (*their; before a noun*)
3. The Martins also recycle theirs. (*theirs; stands alone*)
4. Are these empty cans yours? (*yours; stands alone*)
5. Yes, those are my cans. (*my; before a noun*)

FLUENCY PRACTICE Have volunteers read aloud the announcements they completed in the writing activity.

Interactive Writing: Persuasive Announcement

`RETEACH` Display the draft of an announcement from the Preteach activity. Read it aloud with students. Ask them what changes need to be made to it. Ask: **Have I included all the necessary information? Have I given persuasive reasons?** Discuss students' suggestions for changes or additions to the announcement. Write the revised announcement based on students' suggestions. Then have students revise their own announcements and copy them into their Language Journals.

Grammar-Writing Connection

`RETEACH` Have students work in pairs or in small groups to discuss what it means to share the Earth. Then have students draw pictures to show their ideas. Encourage students to describe their pictures orally. Then work with them to write a sentence or two that describes each picture. Encourage students to use possessive pronouns in their sentences. Check students' writing and suggest any corrections they need to make.

FLUENCY PRACTICE Have students use the illustration on page 13 to retell part of "Kids Care." Encourage them to use as many vocabulary words and concept words as possible.

Name _____

Find four words from "Kids Care" that are new to you. Write one of the words on each short line below. Draw a picture in the box to help you remember the word. Then write a sentence using the word.

1.
Word: _____

Sentence: _____

_____

2.
Word: _____

Sentence: _____

_____

3.
Word: _____

Sentence: _____

_____

4.
Word: _____

Sentence: _____

_____

© Harcourt

TO THE TEACHER Remind students that picture is a type of graphic aid. It may help them understand new information. Then model associating a new word with a picture. Discuss how the picture helps them remember the word and its meaning.

LESSON 15

Use with "The Case of the Flying Saucer People"

BEFORE

Building Background and Vocabulary

Build Background/Access Prior Knowledge

Ask students to discuss what they know about the moon. Ask: **What things have you heard about the moon that are facts? What things have you heard about the moon that are fantasy?** Record students' responses in a chart like this.

Facts About the Moon	Fantasies About the Moon
The moon causes tides.	There is a "man in the moon."
The moon is covered with craters.	The moon is made of green cheese.
Astronauts have visited the moon.	A full moon makes people act strangely.

Selection Vocabulary

PRETEACH Display Teaching Transparency 143, and read the words aloud. Then point to the picture as you read the following sentences.

1. This is a **publicity** poster. It advertises a movie.
2. This is the **translation** of the title. It tells what the French title means in English.
3. Your eyes, nose, and mouth are all facial **features**.
4. This man has **piercing** eyes. They seem to look right through you.
5. The movie will be shown without **subtitles** for advanced French students. They know the language so well that they don't need them.

AFTER

Building Background and Vocabulary

Selection Vocabulary

RETEACH Revisit Teaching Transparency 143. Read the words with students. Have students work in pairs to discuss the meanings of the words and to answer questions such as: Do a person's **features** tell how the person looks or how the person acts? Does a **translation** tell how words sound or what words mean?

Write the following sentence frames on the board. Read each frame, and ask students to choose a vocabulary word to complete it. Write students' responses in the blanks.

1. This restaurant gets a lot of good _____. (*publicity*)
2. The menu is written in Chinese. I will ask for a _____. (*translation*)
3. Ana has lovely facial _____. (*features*)
4. The man has _____ black eyes. (*piercing*)
5. The _____ students was able to start college two years early.

Have student write these words in their Language Dictionaries.

FLUENCY PRACTICE Have students read the completed sentence frames aloud. Encourage them to describe the illustrations on Teaching Transparency 143 by using the vocabulary words and any other words they know.

Build Background: "The Case of the Flying Saucer People"

DISTANT VOYAGES

PRETEACH Have students look at the pictures on *Pupil Edition* pages 350–351. Explain that this story is about a man who says that he has traveled to the moon with little people in a flying saucer.

Text Structure: Main Idea and Details

PRETEACH Tell students that writers often organize their ideas by main ideas and supporting details. Remind students that the main idea is not always stated. They may need to identify important details from the story to figure out the main idea.

Write the headings *Main Idea* and *Details* on the board. Tell students to look for the main idea and details in the story as you read it together.

Directed Reading: "The Case of the Flying Saucer People"

RETEACH Use these sentences to walk students through the story.

Pages 350–353

- A man sees a flying saucer with a little person inside.
- Adam, or Einstein, knows a lot about science. He is talking to his mother, a newspaper reporter.
- Einstein's mother is telling him about the man who says he saw a flying saucer.
- The man wants publicity for a book he wrote about the flying saucer people.

Pages 354–355

- This is Mr. Janus, who says he saw the flying saucer and the little people.
- This is Mr. Janus on the moon. Mr. Janus says the little people took him there.

 QUESTIONS: pages 350–355

- Does Mr. Janus say that he went to the moon? (*yes*)
- What does Einstein know a lot about? (*science*)

Pages 356–358

- Mr. Janus says he heard the little people hammering on the moon.
- The little person uses a translation machine to talk to Mr. Janus.

Pages 359–361

- Einstein knows that Mr. Janus's story is not true.
- Einstein is telling his mother that Mr. Janus could not have heard hammering on the moon because the moon has no air for sound to travel through.

 QUESTIONS: pages 356–361

- Does Mr. Janus say that he heard hammering? (*yes*)
- How does Einstein know that Mr. Janus's story is not true? (*Mr. Janus says that he heard hammering, but there is no air on the moon for sound to travel through.*)

FLUENCY PRACTICE Ask a volunteer to read aloud a paragraph from Pupil Edition page 353. Then have students describe the illustration on page 354. Encourage students to use as many vocabulary words as they can.

Build Background: "Walk on the Moon"

PRETEACH Remind students that "The Case of the Flying Saucer People" is about a man who says that he went to the moon. In "Walk on the Moon" students will read about astronauts who really did travel to the moon.

English-
Language
Learners
Book

Write these Concept Words on the board. Use them in sentences.

Concept Words
surface
dust
air
astronaut
travel
visit

- Many rocks cover the **surface** of the moon.
- The surface is also covered with moon **dust**.
- There is no **air**, so people can't breathe.
- An **astronaut** must wear a spacesuit to breathe.
- It takes three days to **travel** to the moon.
- Someday people will **visit** the moon again.

Have students add these words to their Language Dictionaries.

Directed Reading: "Walk on the Moon"

📖 **Summary** *Astronauts who visit the moon must wear spacesuits and learn to move in the moon's weak gravity.*

Use these sentences to walk students through the story.

Pages 2–5
- This is the moon. This photograph of Earth was taken from the moon.
- The surface of the moon is covered with dust. There is no air on the moon.

Pages 6–7
- This is a dog named Laika. He was sent into space by the Soviet Union.
- This is Ham, a chimpanzee. He was sent into space by the United States.
- These astronauts are wearing spacesuits.

QUESTIONS: pages 2–7
- Is there air on the moon? (*no*)
- What covers the surface of the moon? (*dust*)

Pages 8–11
- These astronauts were the first people to walk on the moon. They went to the moon in July of 1969.
- The astronauts used radios to talk to people on Earth.
- This is Neil Armstrong, the first man to walk on the moon.

Pages 12–16
- Alan Shepard is playing golf on the moon!
- This astronaut is playing the flute. Look at the things floating around her.
- Scientists made a car that astronauts could drive on the moon.
- This is a footprint on the moon. There is no wind on the moon.

QUESTIONS: pages 8–16
- Are astronauts able to talk to people on Earth? (*yes*)
- When did the first people visit the moon? (*July, 1969*)

★ **Focus Skill** **Text Structure: Main Idea and Details**

RETEACH Review main idea and details with students. Then ask students to revisit the story to find the main idea and details of "Walk on the Moon."

FLUENCY PRACTICE Ask students to read aloud a paragraph of "Walk on the Moon." Have students use the illustrations on pages 8–9 to retell part of the selection. Encourage them to use concept words.

Interactive Writing: Persuasive Paragraph

PRETEACH Tell students that they are going to work with you to write persuasive paragraphs. Remind students that persuasive writing must convince the reader. Tell students that the audience for their paragraphs will be their classmates. The topic will be "Travel to the moon with me!" Students will try to make their classmates believe that they really are going to the moon and will try to persuade their classmates to come along. Generate a concept web like the one shown with the topic in the center circle. Brainstorm with students persuasive reasons to take a trip to the moon and add them to the web.

Then work with students to state each reason as a complete sentence. Write the sentences on the board. Help students organize the sentences into paragraphs. Tell students to begin each paragraph with a topic sentence that tells the main idea and then add sentences that support the main idea. Encourage students to come to the board and write sentences dictated by the class. Reread the paragraphs frequently for sense.

Grammar: Pronoun Case

PRETEACH Discuss with students that the **case** of a pronoun reflects its use in a sentence. Point out the following:

- A pronoun that acts as a subject is in the **subjective case.**
- A pronoun that acts as an object is in the **objective case.**
- A pronoun that shows possession is in the **possessive case.**

Write the following sentences on the board, and read them aloud:

- *We built a rocket.*
- *Jamal and Gloria will fly it to the moon.*
- *Their trip will be awesome!*

Ask students to identify the pronoun in each sentence. (*We, it, Their*) Then tell students that the pronoun in the first sentence is in the subjective case. In the second sentence the pronoun is in the objective case because it is the object of the sentence. In the third sentence the pronoun is in the possessive case because it shows possession.

Write the following sentences on the board, and read them aloud. Ask students to identify the pronoun and its case in each sentence.

1. Juan asked me to take a trip to the moon. (*me; objective case*)
2. Juan and his sister are going. (*his; possessive case*)
3. Juan's mom gave them permission. (*them; objective case*)
4. She said to be back in time for dinner. (*She; subjective case*)
5. Juan's dad is making pizza, so we will be back. (*we; subjective case*)

FLUENCY PRACTICE Have volunteers read aloud the paragraphs they completed in the writing activity.

Interactive Writing: Persuasive Paragraph

RETEACH Display the completed paragraph from page 89. Read it aloud with students. Ask them what they think needs to changed and why. Ask: **Is the paragraph persuasive? Does it convince you to take a trip to the moon?** Discuss students' suggestions for changing or adding to the paragraph. Write the revised paragraph on the board based on students' suggestions. Then have students copy the revised paragraphs into their Language Journals.

Grammar-Writing Connection

RETEACH Have students work in pairs or in a small group to discuss the two selections they have read in this lesson. Then have students draw pictures to show their favorite part of each one. Encourage students to describe their pictures orally. Then work with them to write a sentence or two that describes their pictures. Ask students to use pronouns and then label them to identify their case. Check students' writing for spelling, punctuation, and grammar and model how to correct any errors.

FLUENCY PRACTICE Have volunteers read aloud their sentences from the Grammar-Writing Connection and share their pictures with the class. Encourage students to explain how they used pronouns in their sentences.

Name _____

Imagine that you really did take a trip to the moon. Draw a comic strip about your trip. Use speech balloons to show what people are saying.

TO THE TEACHER Read aloud the directions with students. Point out how a speech balloon is used in the example provided. Then have students work in pairs to complete the page.

© Harcourt

Use with "Hattie's Birthday Box"

BEFORE

Building Background and Vocabulary

Build Background/Access Prior Knowledge

Invite students to describe a gift they once gave. Ask them to tell what made the gift special. Record students' responses in a chart like this:

Gift I gave	Why It Was Special
bracelet	I made it myself.
book	It was my favorite book.

Selection Vocabulary

PRETEACH Display Teaching Transparency 152 and read the words aloud. Then point to the pictures as you read the following sentences:

1. The man feels **despair**. He has lost all hope. He is very sad.
2. The man **brooded** while his wife looked at their small food supply. He is worried that they will not have enough to eat.
3. The man and the woman would like to **homestead** on the land. They would like to live on the land and grow their own food.
4. The woman is deciding how to make their **rations** last longer. She wants to make their food last as long as possible.
5. The woman **concocted** a plan to make their food last longer. She made up a plan to help her family survive.
6. It is **undeniable** that the man and woman will have to work a lot to farm the land. It is plainly true that farming will be very hard.
7. The bird watched the people from its **perch**. It is sitting on a high seat.

AFTER

Building Background and Vocabulary

Selection Vocabulary

RETEACH Revisit Teaching Transparency 152. Read the words with students. Have students discuss the meanings of the words and answer questions such as: *Does* **despair** *mean "hopeful" or "hopeless"?*

Write the following sentence frames on the board. Read each frame and ask students to choose a vocabulary word to complete it. Write students' responses in the blanks.

1. My sister feels _____. She thinks she will never see her best friend again. (*despair*)
2. My mother _____ because we were late. She worried (*brooded*)
3. The settlers wanted to _____. They wanted to build a house and to farm the land. (*homestead*)
4. When you do not have a lot of food to eat, you must try make your _____ last longer. (*rations*)
5. Sara _____ a plan to have a surprise party for Ana. (*concocted*)
6. The parrot is sitting on a _____. (*perch*)

Have students write the selection vocabulary words in their Language Dictionaries.

FLUENCY PRACTICE Encourage students to describe the illustrations on Teaching Transparency 152 by using the vocabulary words and any other words they know.

Build Background: "Hattie's Birthday Box"

Revisit the pictures on *Pupil Edition* pages 370-371. Tell students that the man is Spencer, and that his family is having a birthday party for him. Explain that Spencer is nervous about seeing his sister because of a present he gave her a long time ago. Ask students if they have ever been nervous about giving a gift.

DISTANT VOYAGES

Focus Skill Word Relationships

PRETEACH Remind students that when they read an unfamiliar word, they should use context to determine the word's meaning. Explain that this means using the words or sentences that surround an unfamiliar word to figure out the word's meaning. Draw a two-column chart on the board with the headings *Sentence* and *Meaning*. Above the chart write *spring*. Under *Sentence* write *He taught her to swim in the cool spring.* Ask students for possible meanings of *spring* (*season of the year, to jump, spring water*). Read the sentence aloud and point out that the author uses the word *swim* to give the reader context to understand the meaning of *spring*. Write the correct definition for *spring* (*water*), and write it on the board under the heading *Meaning*. After students have read the story, write the following under *Sentence: Flowers grow in the spring.* Ask students to define *spring* (*season of the year*), and write it under *Meaning*. Point out that the word *flowers* gives the reader context to figure out the meaning of *spring*.

Pages 370–375

 QUESTIONS: pages 370–375

Pages 376–380

 QUESTIONS: pages 376–380

Directed Reading: "Hattie's Birthday Box"

RETEACH Use these sentences to walk students through the story.
- This is Spencer McClintic. He is 100 years old today.
- Spencer's great-great granddaughter calls him Grandaddy.
- Spencer tells of the day that his sister Hattie got married.
- When Spencer and Hattie were younger, they were very good friends.
- Before Hattie left, Spencer gave her a special box that he had made for her. It had her initials on the top.
- How old is Spencer? (*100 years old*)
- What is Spencer's sister's name? (*Hattie*)
- What did Spencer give his sister when she went away? (*He gave her a box with her initials on the top.*)
- There are lots of people at the party. Hattie arrives at the party.
- Grandaddy and Hattie are hugging. They both look happy.
- The box Spencer gave to Hattie was empty.
- Are there many people at the party, or just a few? (*many*)
- What do Spencer and Hattie do when they see each other? (*hug*)
- What was in the box that Spencer gave Hattie? (*Nothing—the box was empty.*)

FLUENCY PRACTICE Ask a volunteer to read a paragraph from *Pupil Edition* page 377 aloud.

Build Background: "Time for a Play"

PRETEACH Remind students that "Hattie's Birthday Box" is about Spencer, a man who is nervous about seeing his sister at his birthday party. In "Time for a Play," students will read about Han, a girl who is nervous about what will happen at school.

English-Language Learners Book

Concept Words
play
part
props
memorize

Write the concept words on the board. Use them in sentences to illustrate their meanings.

- The class put on the **play** "Cinderella." Han acted the **part** of Cinderella.
- The class used a glass slipper and a crown as **props** for the play.
- Han tried very hard to **memorize** her lines so that she would not forget them.

Have students add the concept words to their Language Dictionaries.

Directed Reading: "Time for a Play"

📖 **Summary** *Han suggests that her class put on a play for the Valentine's Day competition. The class decides to do the play "Cinderella." Han acts the part of Cinderella. The class wins the competition.*

Use these sentences to walk students through the story.

Pages 2–5
- Han is talking to her mother and father at dinnertime.
- Han's teacher asks the class what they would like to do for the competition.
- At home, Han thinks of something interesting for her class to do.

Pages 6–7
- Han tells the teacher she wants to do a play.
- Han's classmates are talking about what play to put on.

❓ QUESTIONS: pages 2–7
- Is Han a new student at the school? (*yes*)
- What special day is the school celebrating? (*Valentine's Day*)
- How does Han feel when she suggests the class put on a play? (*nervous*)

Pages 8–11
- Here are Han's parents. They are happy that Han will make new friends.
- Han's friends are happy that she will play the part of Cinderella.
- Han tells her parents the good news.

Pages 12–16
- Han and her friends are practicing for the play. Han uses a shawl as a prop.
- The students practice in the auditorium with their props.
- Han is wearing the pretty shawl, and a boy is giving her a glass slipper.
- Han's class wins the competition.

❓ QUESTIONS: pages 8–16
- How does the class feel about putting on a play? (*excited*)
- What are the props that the class uses? (*glass slipper, crown, shawl*)
- What happens at the end of the story? (*Han's class wins the competition.*)

★ Focus Skill Word Relationships

RETEACH Review the use of context to determine word meaning with students. Then write the word *play* on the board. Ask students to suggest possible meanings of the word. (*fun activity, comedy* or *drama on stage*) Then write this sentence on the board: *I was thinking we could put on a play for the Valentine's Day competition.* Ask students to revisit the story to explain what the word *play* means in this sentence. Write the correct definition on the board. (*comedy* or *drama on stage*)

FLUENCY PRACTICE Have students use the illustration on page 16 to retell part of "Time for a Play."

Interactive Writing: Paragraph That Compares

PRETEACH Tell students they are going to work with you to write a paragraph in which they compare themselves to Han from "Time for a Play." Generate a Venn diagram with *Han* written in one circle and *I* in the other circle. In the area where the circles intersect, write, *want to make new friends*. Then have students brainstorm additional words or phrases which compare themselves to Han. Write their suggestions on the board where the circles intersect.

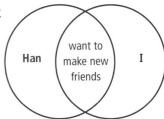

Using the diagram, work with students to develop sentences in which they compare themselves to Han. Write the sentences on the board. Have students help you arrange the sentences in logical order and write a draft of a paragraph that compares on the board. Have students copy the draft on their lap boards or in their notebooks.

Grammar: Reflexive Pronouns

PRETEACH Discuss the definition of a reflexive pronoun with students. Point out the following:

- A **reflexive pronoun** generally refers to the subject of a sentence or a clause.
- *Myself, yourself, himself, herself,* and *itself* are **singular reflexive pronouns.** *Ourselves, yourselves,* and *themselves* are the **plural forms.**

Write the following sentences on the board and read them aloud:

- *Han and her classmates made the props by themselves.*
- *Han memorized her lines by herself.*
- *Han felt good about herself after the play.*

Tell students that reflexive pronouns can be used only when the pronoun refers to the subject. In the first sentence, *themselves* refers to Han and her classmates. In the second and third sentences, *herself* refers to Han.

Read the following sentences aloud. Ask students to restate each sentence, adding the word *by* and a reflexive pronoun:

1. Han made new friends. (*Han made new friends by herself.*)
2. The students practiced the play. (*The students practiced the play by themselves.*)
3. Han thought of an idea. (*Han thought of an idea by herself.*)
4. The students took their places on the stage. (*The students took their places on the stage by themselves.*)

FLUENCY PRACTICE Have volunteers read aloud the paragraph that they drafted in the writing activity.

Interactive Writing: Paragraph That Compares

RETEACH Display the draft of the paragraph that compares from the Preteach activity. Read it aloud with students. Ask students what changes they would make to it. Discuss students' suggestions for changes or additions to the paragraph. Write the revised paragraph based on students' suggestions. Then have students copy the revised paragraph into their Language Journals.

Grammar-Writing Connection

RETEACH Write these sentences on the board and read them aloud with students:

- *Han would feel embarrassed about herself if the other students laughed at her.*
- *Han worked hard by herself to prepare for the play.*
- *Han felt better about herself when the play won the competition.*

Have students work in pairs or in a small group to discuss what they would like their class to do to celebrate Valentine's Day and what they would do to prepare. Then have students draw pictures to show their ideas. Encourage students to describe their pictures orally. Then work with them to write a short paragraph that describes each picture. Encourage students to use reflexive pronouns in their sentences. Remind students that a reflexive pronoun refers to the subject of a sentence or a clause. Check students' writing and suggest any corrections they need to make.

FLUENCY PRACTICE Have students choose a page from "Time for a Play" to read aloud.

Name _____

A Imagine that your class wants to put on a play. Think about the name of a play that you would like to do and what you would need to do to prepare for the play. Write the answers to the questions in the chart below.

What is the name of the play?	
What are the parts in the play?	
What props are needed?	
How would the class prepare for the play?	
How would you feel before you put on the play?	

B Draw a picture of the main character(s) in the play.

TO THE TEACHER Model filling in the chart with information about "Cinderella." Have students read aloud what they wrote in the chart for sense and completeness. Direct students to draw a picture of the main character(s) from the play they've chosen in part A.

Hattie's Birthday Box/Time for a Play • **Lesson 16**   **97**

© Harcourt

Use with "William Shakespeare & the Globe"

BEFORE

Building Background and Vocabulary

Build Background/Access Prior Knowledge

Have students look at the illustrations on *Pupil Edition* pages 396–397. Point to the pictures of the boy in school and the city. Explain that the boy is going to move to the city. Then ask: **Have you ever visited a city? Which one(s)? What are some things that you might find in a city?** Record students responses in a chart like this one.

The City
traffic
buildings
theaters

Selection Vocabulary

PRETEACH Display Teaching Transparency 162, and read the words aloud. Then point to the pictures as you read the following sentences:

1. The theater is very **lavish**. It is very fancy.
2. A man on the stage wants to **dismantle** the scenery. He wants to take apart the decorations on the stage.
3. The theater is **congested**. The theater is full of people.
4. The **shareholder** is happy that there is a big audience. He is one of the owners of the theater and will make a lot of money tonight.
5. A **patron** is sitting in the balcony. She is someone who has given money to the theater.
6. The woman has an **adornment** on her head. It looks like a crown.
7. The man in the balcony is **critical** of the play. He does not like it.

AFTER

Building Background and Vocabulary

Selection Vocabulary

RETEACH Revisit Teaching Transparency 162. Read the words aloud with students. Then have them discuss the meanings of the words and answer questions such as: *Does **critical** mean "likes" or "does not like"?*

Write these sentence frames on the board. Read each one aloud, and ask students to choose a vocabulary word to complete it. Write students' responses in the blanks.

1. My grandmother is a _____ of the art museum. (*patron*)
2. The accident caused the roads to be _____ with cars. (*congested*)
3. Mrs. Simon is _____ of the long movie. (*critical*)
4. I will _____ the scenery after the play and take it off the stage. (*dismantle*)
5. The _____ built a theater and hopes to make money. (*shareholder*)
6. The style is expensive furniture _____ . (*lavish*)
7. The _____ in Maria's hair made her look beautiful. (*adornment*)

Have students write the selection vocabulary words in their Language Dictionaries.

FLUENCY PRACTICE Have students read the sentence frames aloud.

Build Background: "William Shakespeare & the Globe"

DISTANT
VOYAGES

PRETEACH Revisit the pictures on *Pupil Edition* pages 396–397. Tell students that the boy is Will Shakespeare and that he is going to move to a city when he is an adult. Ask students why they think he will move to the city. (*to find work, to write plays*)

Fact and Opinion

Tell students that in some selections they will read both facts and opinions. Explain that a **fact** is something that can be proved. A fact is based on evidence. An **opinion** is a feeling, thought, or belief. Draw a two-column chart on the board with the headings *Fact* and *Opinion.* Tell students that William Shakespeare was an actor and a playwright. Write that information in the *Fact* column. After students have read the story, read aloud the following statements: *William Shakespeare was born in Stratford-upon-Avon* (fact); *Shakespeare is the greatest playwright in the world* (opinion). Ask students under which column each statement should be written.

AFTER

Reading "William Shakespeare & the Globe"

Pages 392–397

Pages 398–399

QUESTIONS:
pages 392–399

Pages 400–403

Pages 404–409

QUESTIONS:
pages 400–409

Directed Reading: "William Shakespeare & the Globe"

RETEACH Use these sentences to walk students through the story.

- William Shakespeare was a famous poet, playwright, and actor in England.
- This is the Globe Theatre. Many of Shakespeare's plays were performed here.
- This is a boy making a model of the Globe.
- This is Will's family. They lived in Stratford-upon-Avon in England.
- London Bridge had houses, shops, and a church.
- Queen Elizabeth I. liked to watch plays. Notice her lavish clothes.
- Clowns and acrobats also entertained people.
- Did Will Shakespeare's family live in London? (*no*)
- What did the city of London have? (*bridge, houses, shops, churches*)
- What did Queen Elizabeth and the English people like to watch? (*plays*)
- Here are a few of the theatres built for actors.
- These are famous clowns, who were also poets, playwrights, and musicians.
- The actors secretly dismantled the Theatre where Will worked. They took the theater apart and moved it across the river to rebuild it.
- This is the inside of the Globe Theatre. It became very successful.
- The Globe caught on fire one day. It burned to the ground.
- Will died on his fifty-second birthday. He became famous for his plays.
- Was William Shakespeare a famous playwright? (*yes*)
- What was a name of a famous theatre? (*the Globe*)
- What happened to the Globe Theatre? (*It burned to the ground.*)

FLUENCY PRACTICE Encourage students to use vocabulary words to describe the illustration on *Pupil Edition* page 397.

BEFORE

Making
Connections
pages 418–419

Build Background: "City Builders"

PRETEACH Remind students that "William Shakespeare & the Globe" is about Will, a man who moves to the city to find work as an actor and playwright. In "City Builders," students will read about cities.

English-
Language
Learners
Book

Write the concept words on the board. Use them in sentences to illustrate their meanings.

Concept Words
bridge
entertainment
skyscrapers
neighborhood
traffic
roads

- We used the **bridge** to cross the river.
- The city has a lot of **entertainment**. You can go to movies and plays.
- New York city has many **skyscrapers**. They are very tall buildings.
- I like the **neighborhood** where my family lives.
- There are many cars and trucks on the highway. There is a lot of **traffic**.
- The **roads** in the city bring people to and from their houses and work.

Have students add the concept words to their Language Dictionaries.

AFTER

Skill Review
pages 420–421

Directed Reading: "City Builders"

📖 **Summary** *Cities are busy places with lots of things to do. City planners work to make life in a city better. The cities of London and Washington, D.C., are examples of the kind of work city planners do.*

Use these sentences to walk students through the story.

Pages 2–4
- The first cities were built thousands of years ago.
- Big cities have office buildings, stores, and skyscrapers.

Pages 4–7
- Going to a play or a movie is a fun thing to do at night in a city.
- City planners are people who know how to plan and build cities.
- City planners try to make life better for people who live in cities.

❓ QUESTIONS:
pages 2–7
- Are all cities new? (no)
- What is there to do at night in a city? (walk, shop, go to movies or plays)
- What do city planners do? (They look for ways to make cities better.)

Pages 8–11
- This city planner is answering questions about new plans for the city.
- The city planners check the work being done to make sure it is right.

Pages 12–16
- This is London. It has been the biggest city in England for four hundred years.
- In old London, the roads were crowded. Trash made the city smell bad.
- Washington, D.C., is the capital city of the United States.
- Orlando, Florida, is a modern city. Many people live and work there.
- Some city planners have to solve problems like rebuilding roads and bridges.

❓ Questions:
pages 8–16
- Which large English city is four hundred years old? (*London*)
- Why did the city of Orlando grow so fast? (*Disney World was built on the edge of Orlando. People needed more places to live.*)

(Focus Skill) Fact and Opinion

Review the definitions of fact and opinion with students. Then draw on the board a two-column chart with the headings *Fact* and *Opinion*. Ask students to revisit the story to find information to add under each heading. Record students' findings on the chart.

FLUENCY PRACTICE Have students use the illustration on page 3 to retell part of "City Builders."

Interactive Writing: News Story

PRETEACH Tell students that the story "William Shakespeare & the Globe" presents information about events. Explain that a news story also presents information about events. Tell students that they are going to work with you to write a news story about something new that has happened in their school or class. Brainstorm with students some possible topics for the news story. Then have them select a topic to write about. Write on the board the following question words: *Who? What? When? How? Why?*

Who?
What?
When?
How?
Why?

Work with students to formulate a question using one of the question words. Then model a possible answer for it. Then have students work in small groups to formulate additional questions and answers. Write students' questions and answers on the board. Using those answers, write a draft of a short news story on the board or on chart paper.

Grammar: Adjectives and Articles

PRETEACH Discuss the definition of an adjective with students. Point out the following:

- An **adjective** describes a noun or a pronoun.
- Adjectives can tell what kind, how many, or which one.
- An adjective may come before the noun it describes. It may also follow a verb such as *is, seems,* or *appears*.
- The adjectives *a, an*, and *the* are called **articles.**
- Use *a* before a word that begins with a consonant sound.
- Use *an* before a word that begins with a vowel sound.

Write the following sentences on the board and read them aloud:

- *William Shakespeare was an actor.*
- *He was also a playwright.*
- *He moved to the city of London.*

Tell students that the adjectives *an* and *a* in the first two sentences describe William Shakespeare. The adjective *the* in the third sentence describes the city of London.

Write the following sentences frames on the board and read them aloud. Ask students to restate each sentence, using the article *a* or *an* where appropriate. Write their responses in the blanks.

1. _____ city can be a nice place to live. (*A*)
2. _____ tall building is called _____ skyscraper. (*A, a*)
3. We saw _____ interesting play. (*an*)
4. The city planners want to build _____ new road. (*a*)
5. I live in _____ apartment. (*an*)

FLUENCY PRACTICE Have volunteers read aloud the news story they drafted in the writing activity.

Interactive Writing: News Story

RETEACH Display the draft of the news story from the Preteach activity. Read it aloud with students. Ask students what changes they would make to it and why. Discuss students' suggestions for changes or additions to the story. Write a revised news story based on students' suggestions. Then have students copy the revised story into their Language Journals.

Grammar-Writing Connection

RETEACH Write these sentences on the board and read them aloud with students:

- *I would like to live in a city.*
- *I would not like to live in a city.*

Have students work in pairs or in small groups to discuss their opinions about living in a city. Ask students to come up with reasons and facts to support their opinions. Have students choose one of the reasons to use as a topic sentence for a short paragraph. Encourage students to use adjectives when writing why they would or would not like to live in a city. Remind students that the adjectives *a, and,* and *the* are articles. Point out that *a* is used before a word that begins with a consonant sound and *an* is used before a word that begins with a vowel sound. Check students' writing, and suggest any corrections they need to make.

FLUENCY PRACTICE Have students choose a page from "City Builders" to read aloud.

Name _____

Think about the news story you wrote about something new that has happened in your school. Imagine that you are going to publish your story in a newspaper. Make up a headline for the story, and write it on the line below. Then draw a picture below to go with your story.

Headline: _____

TO THE TEACHER Explain to students that the purpose of a headline is to attract the reader's attention. Provide students with several examples of headlines from local newspapers. Remind students to read aloud their headlines for sense.

William Shakespeare & the Globe/City Builders • Lesson 17 **103**

© Harcourt

Use with "The World of William Joyce Scrapbook"

BEFORE

Building Background and Vocabulary

Build Background/Access Prior Knowledge

Point to an illustration in the classroom, and ask students if they like to draw. Have volunteers share information about what kinds of things they like to draw. Ask: **Are they imaginary things? Real things? Animals? People?** Ask students if they ever write stories to go with their drawings.

Selection Vocabulary

PRETEACH Display Teaching Transparency 171 and read the words aloud. Then point to the pictures as you read the following sentences:

1. The girl is making a **series** of drawings. She is making many drawings.
2. The girl is drawing with **charcoal**. It makes the drawing black.
3. The girl has **pastels**. These will make different colors in the drawing.
4. The girl is **illustrating**. She is drawing a picture.
5. The man **encouraged** the girl. He wants her to draw more.

AFTER

Building Background and Vocabulary

Selection Vocabulary

RETEACH Revisit Teaching Transparency 171. Read the words with students. Have students work in pairs to discuss the meanings of the words and to answer questions such as: Does **series** mean *many* or *one*? Does **charcoal** make *different colors* or *black*?

Write the following sentence frames on the board. Read each sentence and ask students to choose a vocabulary word to complete it. Write students' responses in the blanks.

1. We are drawing a _____ of pictures about dogs. (*series*)
2. I want to make my drawing black, so I will use _____. (*charcoal*)
3. If you want to have different colors in your drawing, you should use _____. (*pastels*)
4. I like _____ stories because my pictures make them interesting. (*illustrating*)
5. My teacher _____ me to make more drawings. (*encouraged*)

Have students write these words in their Language Dictionaries.

FLUENCY PRACTICE Have students read the sentence frames aloud. Encourage them to describe the illustrations on Teaching Transparency 171 using the vocabulary words and any other words they know.

Build Background: "The World of William Joyce Scrapbook"

Have students look at the illustrations on *Pupil Edition* pages 424–425. Tell students that the artist who made the drawings is William Joyce. Explain that William Joyce is going to talk about how he makes his drawings. Discuss with students what materials they use to make drawings. (*charcoal, pastels,*)

DISTANT
VOYAGES

 Synonyms and Antonyms

PRETEACH Discuss with students that words that have the same or similar meanings as other words (*such as big and large*) are called *synonyms.* Then explain that there are words that have opposite meanings (*such as big and little*) called *antonyms.* Draw two lists on the board with the labels *Synonyms* and *Antonyms.* Tell students that *illustrating* and *drawing* are synonyms. Then tell students that *real* and *made-up* are antonyms. Write these words on the lists. After you have read the story, ask students to revisit the text to find more words that are *synonyms* and *antonyms.* Add these words to the lists.

Reading
"The World of
William Joyce
Scrapbook"

Pages 424–425
Pages 426–427

Pages 428–429

Questions:
pages 424–429
Pages 430–431

Pages 432–433

Page 434
Questions:
pages 430–434

Directed Reading: "The World of William Joyce Scrapbook"

RETEACH Use these bulleted sentences to walk students through the story.

- This is William Joyce. His job is to write stories and draw pictures.
- He draws pictures of real things and of made-up things.
- William explains how he draws every day using ideas already in his head.
- Here are pictures of William as a kid.
- When he read and watched TV, it got his imagination working.
- Here are some of William's first pictures.
- He learned how to draw by looking at other people's drawings.
- Soon he found his own way to draw.
- Does William Joyce draw pictures? (*yes*)
- How often does William draw pictures? (*every day*)
- William explains how he makes a book by putting pencil sketches together.
- He tells about the first book he ever wrote, "George Shrinks."
- William tells about the dinosaur books he wrote.
- He tells how he made the story.
- William is working at his desk at home.
- Did William write a book about a dinosaur? (*yes*)
- Where does William work? (*at home; at his desk*)

FLUENCY PRACTICE Ask a volunteer to read the paragraph from page 433 aloud. Encourage students to describe the illustrations on Pupil Edition 432–433 using as many vocabulary words as they can in their descriptions.

BEFORE

Making
Connections
pages 436–437

Concept Words
imagination
shapes
real
flat
round
lines

Build Background: "You Are an Artist"

PRETEACH Remind students that "The World of William Joyce Scrapbook" is about William, an artist who talks about how he draws. Tell students that in "You Are an Artist," they will read about how to make their own pictures better. Ask students what materials they would need to have in order to draw.

English-Language Learners Book

Write the concept words on the board. Use them in sentences to illustrate their meanings.

- You use your **imagination** when you draw.
- You can draw **shapes**, such as circles, squares and triangles.
- I want my pictures of the houses to look as **real** as they can.
- A square is **flat**. It looks smooth when you draw it.
- A circle is **round**. It has a curved shape.
- I drew a picture and wrote a story on the **lines** above it.

Have students add these words to their Language Dictionaries

AFTER

Skill Review
pages 438–439

Directed Reading: "You Are an Artist"

📖 **Summary** *Artists need to practice to make better pictures. This selection walks the reader through basic tools that an artist uses. Then it explains how to draw shapes and make the drawings look better.*

Use these sentences to walk students through the story.

Pages 2–5
- You have to practice to make better pictures.
- Before you start to draw, you need paper, pencils, crayons, pastels, and pens.
- You can draw the shapes that you see in a room.
- Your picture doesn't have to look like anything real.

Pages 6–7
- You can learn special ways to draw objects to make them look real.
- Artists use lines to make things look more real.

❓ QUESTIONS: pages 2–7
- Do you have to practice to make better drawings? (*yes*)
- How can you make your drawings of shapes look more real? (*use lines*)

Pages 8–11
- To make a round object look real, use lighter and darker colors.
- You can draw a bowl to make it look real.
- To practice, look at the object that you want to draw and study it carefully.

Pages 12–16
- You can draw a picture of a group of objects called a still-life.
- You can draw a picture of a face.
- You can make pictures look real.
- You can keep a notebook of your drawings and ideas.

❓ QUESTIONS: pages 8–16
- Can you use darker and lighter colors to make a round shape look real? (*yes*)
- How do you draw real things? (*look at it, study it*)

⭐ (Focus Skill) Synonyms and Antonyms

RETEACH Review synonyms and antonyms with students. Then draw on the board two lists with the labels Synonyms and Antonyms. Ask students to revisit the story to suggest some word pairs to include in the lists.

FLUENCY PRACTICE Ask students to read page 13 of "You Are an Artist" aloud. Have students use the illustration on page 15 to retell part of "You Are an Artist" using as many vocabulary and concept words as possible.

Independent Writing: Compare and Contrast

PRETEACH Remind students that William Joyce from "The World of William Joyce Scrapbook" writes stories and draws pictures. In "You Are an Artist" they learned of ways to make their drawings better. Tell students that they are going to write a paragraph comparing and contrasting these two stories. Label one side of the diagram *"The World of William Joyce Scrapbook"* and the other side *"You Are an Artist."* Have students work in small groups to generate similarities and differences to fill in their Venn diagrams.

"The World of William Joyce Scrapbook" **both** "You Are an Artist"

Now have students write a compare and contrast paragraph. Encourage them to use their Venn diagrams to help them organize their ideas. Have students reread frequently to check for sense.

Grammar: Proper Adjectives

Discuss the definition of a *proper adjective* with students. Point out the following:

- A **proper adjective** is formed from a proper noun.
- Many proper adjectives describe nationalities or locations.
- Proper adjectives are formed in a variety of ways.
- Proper adjectives always begin with a capital letter.

Write the following sentences on the board and read them aloud:

- They live in Mexico. They are Mexican.
- They live in Spain. They are Spanish.
- They live in France. They are French.

Using a map or a globe, point to the country mentioned in each sentence and say its name. Then say the *proper adjective* for a citizen of that country.

Write the following sentences on the board or chart paper. Read the following sentences aloud. Ask students to identify the proper adjective in each sentence and correct the spelling.

1. The artist is english. (*English*)
2. I met many Mexico students in my drawing class. (*Mexican*)
3. My friend made a drawing of italian food. (*Italian*)
4. I drew a picture of my vietnamese friend. (*Vietnamese*)
5. The artist illustrated the spains story. (*Spanish*)

FLUENCY PRACTICE Have volunteers read aloud the compare and contrast paragraph they completed in the writing activity.

Independent Writing: Compare and Contrast

RETEACH Have volunteers read their compare and contrast paragraphs aloud. Ask students what they would like to change about it and why. Us the following questions as a guide:

- Did you group all of your similarities together?
- Did you group all of your differences together?
- Which part of your paragraph do you want to emphasize the most? Put it last.

Have students revise their paragraphs. Encourage them to use supporting details from the stories. Then have them copy their revised paragraphs into their Language Journals.

Grammar-Writing Connection

RETEACH Write these sentences on the board and read them aloud with students:

My Scottish friend Kim loves Italian food.

My sister combed my hair into a French braid.

Our family took a trip to a British colony.

Ask students to identify the proper adjectives in the sentences above. Remind them that a proper adjective describes nationalities or locations and that it begins with a capital letter. Then, have students work in pairs or in a small group to write sentences about their friends or places they've been. You may want to have students draw a picture that illustrates one of their sentences. Check students' writing and suggest any corrections they need to make.

FLUENCY PRACTICE Have students read aloud the sentences they wrote in the grammar activity.

Name _____

Cut out these words. First use them to make as many word pairs of synonyms as you can. Then use the words to make as many word pairs of antonyms as you can.

drawing	light	little	round
kid	illustrating	dark	small
real	flat	child	big
large	made-up	circular	imaginary

TO THE TEACHER Have students cut apart copies of these word cards. Ask pairs of students to form synonym and antonym pairs from the cards. You may want to model forming a synonym pair such as *little* and *small*. Have students read their word pairs aloud. Not all words will have both a synonym and an antonym.

© Harcourt

LESSON 19

Use with "Satchmo's Blues"

BEFORE

Building
Background
and Vocabulary

Build Background/Access Prior Knowledge

Have students look at the illustrations on *Pupil Edition* pages 442–443. Point to the boy holding the horn and tell students that he wants to buy his own horn. Then ask: **Where do you go to buy something? How do you get the money to buy it?** Record their responses in a chart like the one shown.

I buy things at	with money that
the market	I save.
the store	my parents give to me.
the restaurant	I get from a job.

Selection Vocabulary

PRETEACH Display Teaching Transparency 180, and read the words aloud. Then point to the pictures as you read the following sentences.

1. The people have **errands** to do. They have to make some short trips to carry out a task, such as buying food or going to the bank.
2. Some people are buying **produce** in the market. They want to buy fruit and vegetables.
3. Other people are going to the **pawnshop**. It is a place where they can exchange their own things for money.
4. The people are visiting the **international** shops. They can find things from different countries, or nations, in these shops.
5. There are **numerous**, or many, people in the shops.
6. This clerk has a **gravelly** voice. He sounds harsh when he talks.

AFTER

Building
Background
and Vocabulary

Selection Vocabulary

RETEACH Revisit Teaching Transparency 180. Read the words with students. Have students discuss the meanings of the words and answer questions such as: *Does **numerous** mean "many" or "few"?*

Write the following sentence frames on the board. Read each one and ask students to choose a vocabulary word to complete it. Write students' responses in the blanks.

1. She has many _____ to do at the bank and the mall. *(errands)*
2. Lu took his bike to the _____ so that he could get some money. *(pawnshop)*
3. The city has many _____ restaurants with Mexican, Chinese, and Indian food. *(international)*
4. Here is the _____ I bought. I got apples and pears. *(produce)*
5. Mr. Gomez has a _____ voice. *(gravelly)*
6. There are many, or _____, shops in the city. *(numerous)*

Have students write the selection vocabulary words in their Language Dictionaries.

FLUENCY PRACTICE Have students read the sentence frames aloud.

Build Background: "Satchmo's Blues"

Revisit the pictures on *Pupil Edition* pages 442–443. Tell students that the boy is Louis Armstrong. Explain that Louis wants to earn money to buy his own horn. Ask students to tell about a time when they saved to purchase something.

DISTANT
VOYAGES

Focus Skill Fact and Opinion

PRETEACH Tell students that sometimes an author presents information as fact, and sometimes as opinion. Explain that a **fact** is a piece of information that can be proved. An **opinion** expresses someone's feeling or ideas about something. Also explain that you may form a **supported inference** about an idea after reading factual evidence that supports the idea. Draw a three-column chart on the board with the headings *Fact*, *Opinion*, and *Supported Inference*. Tell students that the sentence *Louis Armstrong lives in New Orleans* is a fact. Write the sentence in the chart. After students have read the selection, ask them to return to find facts, opinions, and to make supported inferences. Write students' suggestions in the chart.

Directed Reading: "Satchmo's Blues"

RETEACH Use these sentences to walk students through the story.

Pages 442–445

- This is Louis Armstrong. He lives in New Orleans.
- Louis dreams of playing an instrument called the cornet, or *horn*.
- Louis and his family live in the "back o' town."
- Louis wants to buy a cornet, but he doesn't have the money to buy one.
- One day Louis sees a used cornet in a store. It costs $5.

Pages 446–447

- Louis tries to play his friend Santiago's horn, but he can't make a note.
- Louis begins practicing how to play a horn using just his lips.

QUESTIONS: pages 442–447

- Does Louis want to play an instrument? *(yes)*
- What instrument does Louis want to play? *(a cornet or horn)*
- Why can't Louis buy a cornet? *(He doesn't have enough money.)*

Pages 448–451

- Louis finds chores to do around town to earn money.
- Louis's Mama asks him for a quarter for his sister's birthday dinner.
- Louis wants the money to buy his horn, but he gives it to his Mama.
- Louis's Mama thanks him for contributing. She hands Louis a dollar.
- Now he can buy the horn.

Pages 452–455

- Louis goes to the store to buy his used horn.
- Louis plays his horn and makes clear notes. He points his horn to the sky and plays.

QUESTIONS: pages 448–455

- Does Louis get his horn? *(yes)*
- What does Louis need to earn to buy the horn? *(money)*
- Why does Louis's Mama ask him for a quarter? *(She needs money for a special birthday dinner for Louis's sister.)*

FLUENCY PRACTICE Ask a volunteer to read a paragraph from *Pupil Edition* page 449 aloud.

Build Background: "Money, Money, Money"

PRETEACH Remind students that "Satchmo's Blues" is about Louis Armstrong, a boy who wants to buy a horn. In "Money, Money, Money," they will read how people work to earn money.

English-
Language
Learners
Book

Write the concept words on the board. Use them in sentences to illustrate their meanings.

Concept Words
trade
coins
dollar bills
price

- I will *trade*, quarters and other **coins** to buy candy.
- My parents gave me some **dollar bills** to buy something special.
- The **price** of the toy is too high, and I don't have enough money to buy it.

Have students add the concept words to their Language Dictionaries

Directed Reading: "Money, Money, Money"

📖 **Summary** *People have different ways of getting something they want. Some make a trade. Others buy things in a store. People trade their work for money. They use the money to pay for the things.*

Pages 2–5
- Some Native Americans traded things for something they needed or wanted.
- In markets in other countries, the buyer and the seller can decide the price.
- In the United States, each thing in a store has a price.

Pages 6–7
- People trade their work to get money.
- People then trade some of their money for things they need.

❓ QUESTIONS:
pages 2–7
- Do people trade things for something they need? *(yes)*
- When you buy somthing, what do you use? *(dollar bills and coins)*
- How do people get money? *(They trade their work to get money.)*

Pages 8–11
- Dollar bills in the United States are made of paper. Coins are made of metal.
- The coins and bills in the United States have pictures and words on them.

Pages 12–16
- The United States government began making these quarters in 1999.
- The back of each quarter is different. Each of the 50 states will decide what the back of the new quarter will look like.
- This is a new one-dollar coin.
- A picture of an Indian woman, Sacagawea, and her baby is on the front.
- You can trade money, give it as a gift, or save it.

❓ QUESTIONS:
pages 8–16
- Are coins made of paper? *(no)*
- What can you do with money to get something you want or need? *(You can trade money for something you want or need.)*

⭐(Focus Skill) **Fact and Opinion**

RETEACH Write the following sentences on the board:

- *It is a good idea to save your money.*
- *The one-dollar bill has a picture of a bald eagle on the back.*

Have students identify which statement is a fact and which one is an opinion. Then write: *You don't have enough money to buy what you want.* Ask students to form a supported inference based upon the facts in the sentence. *(You need to save money. You can't buy what you want now.)*

> **FLUENCY PRACTICE** Have students use the illustration on page 16 to retell part of "Money, Money, Money."

Interactive Writing: Response to Literature

PRETEACH Tell students that they are going to work with you to write a paragraph about what they liked about the story "Satchmo's Blues." Generate a concept web with the phrase *What I liked about "Satchmo's Blues"* in the center. Have students generate ideas to write in the circles surrounding the web. Write their suggestions in the web.

Model writing a draft of the paragraph. As you do, use these steps to think aloud the process:

- Introduce Louis and explain what problem he faced.
- Discuss how Louis solved his probelm.
- Use the concept web to organize your ideas.

As you work with students to draft their personal responses, encourage them to reread their sentences frequently to make sure they make sense and that complete.

Grammar: Comparing with Adjectives

PRETEACH Point out the following about adjectives that compare:

- **Adjectives** can be used to compare people, places, things, or ideas.
- Some adjectives have special forms for comparing.
- Add -*er* to most adjectives to compare one thing with one other thing. Add -*est* to most adjectives to compare one thing with two or with more things.
- For adjectives of two or more syllables, use *more* instead of –*er* and *most* instead of -*est*. The word *the* often comes before *most*.

Write the following sentences on the board and read them aloud:

- *The one-dollar coin is the largest coin.*
- *The most important people are on coins and bills.*
- *The dime is smaller than the nickel.*

Tell students that the adjectives in the first and the second sentences are used to compare one thing with two or more things. (*largest; most impor-tant*) The adjective in the third sentence is used to compare one thing with one other thing. (*smaller*)

Read the following sentences aloud. Ask students to say whether each adjective compares one thing with one other thing or two or more things. Then have them say the correct adjective.

1. Louis Armstrong was one of the _____ (*great*) musicians. *(two or more; greatest)*
2. Louis became a _____ (*hard*) worker to save money. *(one; harder)*
3. The story about young Louis is the _____ (*interesting*) story that I have read. *(two or more; most interesting)*
4. After he practiced, it was _____ (*easy*) to blow the horn. *(one; easier)*

> **FLUENCY PRACTICE** Have volunteers read aloud the response to literature that they drafted in the writing activity.

Interactive Writing: Response to Literature

RETEACH Display the draft of the paragraph you wrote in the Preteach activity. Read it aloud with students. Ask them what changes they would make to it and the reasons for the changes. Discuss students' suggestions for changes or additions to the paragraph. Write the revised paragraph based on students' suggestions. Then have students copy the revised paragraph into their Language Journals.

Grammar-Writing Connection

RETEACH Write these sentences on the board and read them aloud with students:

- *Louis Armstrong saved a larger amount of money than he needed.*
- *The most important thing you can do is save your money.*

Have students identify the comparative adjectives in the above sentences. (*larger; most important*) Then have students work in pairs or in a small group to discuss good money-saving habits. Ask students to draw pictures to show their ideas. Encourage students to describe their pictures aloud. Then work with them to write a sentence or two that describes their picture. Remind students to use adjectives that compare in their sentences. Check students' writing and suggest any corrections they need to make.

FLUENCY PRACTICE Have students choose a page from "Money, Money, Money" to read aloud.

Name _____

Cut out these pictures and use them to tell a story. If you need an extra picture, draw it in the blank box. Use as many words as you can.

© Harcourt

TO THE TEACHER Have students cut apart copies of these picture cards. Ask pairs of students to tell a story using the words suggested by the pictures. You may want to model forming a story sentence, such as *Sara wanted to buy a birthday gift for her friend.*

Use with "Evelyn Cisneros: Prima Ballerina"

BEFORE

Building Background and Vocabulary

Build Background/Access Prior Knowledge

Have students look at the picture on *Pupil Edition* page 471. Point to the girl dancing and tell students that she wants to be a dancer when she grows up. Ask students what they would like to be when they grow up. Then ask students to share why they want to do that. Ask: **What do you want to be when you grow up? Why do you want to do that?** Record their responses in a chart like this:

I want to be a _____ when I grow up	because
dancer	music makes me happy.
teacher	I like to help people.
doctor	I like math and science.

Selection Vocabulary

PRETEACH Display Teaching Transparency 189 and read the words aloud. Then point to the pictures as you read the following sentences:

1. The man is a **migrant** worker. He moves around to find work.
2. The **timid** girl is fearful that she will make mistakes.
3. The girl **thrived** after she practiced how to dance.
4. A dancer needs **flexibility** to do this move.
5. The girl is an **apprentice**. She is learning from the man.
6. She wants to **devote** time to dancing.
7. The girl may get a **scholarship** to help pay for classes.

AFTER

Building Background and Vocabulary

Selection Vocabulary

RETEACH Revisit Teaching Transparency 189. Have students work in pairs to discuss the meanings of the words and to answer questions such as: Does **thrived** mean *did poorly* or *did well*?

Write the following sentence frames on the board. Read each sentence and ask students to choose a vocabulary word to complete it. Write students' responses in the blanks.

1. Renata must to _____ a lot of time to studying to become a doctor. (*devote*)
2. I am very _____ , so I do not like to talk in front of my class. (*timid*)
3. The _____ workers came to California to pick grapes. (*migrant*)
4. I bend easily. I have a lot of _____ in my back and legs. (*flexibility*)
5. I _____ in dance class after I learned the basic moves. (*thrived*)
6. By practicing very hard, you can earn a _____.(*scholarship*)
7. An _____ learns from a skilled professional. (*apprentice*)

Have students write these words in their Language Dictionaries.

FLUENCY PRACTICE Have students read the sentence frames aloud. Encourage them to describe the illustrations on Teaching Transparency 189 using the vocabulary words and any other words they know.

Build Background: "Evelyn Cisneros: Prima Ballerina"

DISTANT VOYAGES

Revisit the picture on *Pupil Edition* page 471. Tell students that the girl is Evelyn Cisneros. Explain that Evelyn wants to be a ballet dancer when she grows up. Discuss with students what they can be when they grow up. (*doctor, teacher, dancer*)

⭐ Focus Skill Main Idea and Details

PRETEACH Tell students that good readers look for organizational patterns when they are reading informational text. One kind of organizational pattern is *main idea* and *details*. Students can put together the important details of the story to determine the main idea. Draw a two-column chart on the board with the headings *Main Idea* and *Detail*s. Tell students that the sentence *Evelyn Cisneros has changed since she was a young girl* is a main idea in this story. After students have read the story, complete the chart with supporting details for the main idea.

Directed Reading: "Evelyn Cisneros: Prima Ballerina"

RETEACH Use these sentences to walk students through the story.

Pages 466–471
- This is Evelyn Cisneros. She is a prima ballerina.
- Evelyn grew up in California.
- Here is a picture of Evelyn when she was nine.
- Evelyn was shy so her mother encouraged her to take ballet lessons.

Pages 472–473
- This is a picture of the San Francisco Ballet School.
- Evelyn worked very hard there.
- The next year Evelyn was invited to study ballet in New York City.

**❓ QUESTIONS:
pages466–473**
- Does Evelyn dance? (*yes*)
- What type of dance does Evelyn do? (*ballet*)
- What was Evelyn like when she was nine? (*She was very shy.*)

Pages 474–475
- Evelyn was homesick in New York.
- She joined the San Francisco company when she was just eighteen.
- Here is Evelyn at a rehearsal for a ballet called Sleeping Beauty.

Pages 476–477
- Some of Evelyn's performances were broadcast on television.
- Evelyn had some sad times, too, but she got through them.
- Soon she was prima ballerina for the San Francisco Ballet.

Pages 478–480
- Evelyn never forgot her Hispanic heritage.
- Evelyn went from being a shy little girl to being an international star.

**❓ QUESTIONS:
pages 474–480**
- Did Evelyn become a professional dancer? (*yes*)
- In what city did Evelyn dance? (*San Francisco*)

FLUENCY PRACTICE Ask a volunteer to read a paragraph from page 470 aloud. Encourage students to describe the picture on *Pupil Edition* page 472 using as many vocabulary words as they can.

Build Background: "I Want to Be Me"

PRETEACH Remind students that "Evelyn Cisneros: Prima Ballerina" is about a girl who worked very hard to become a dancer. "I Want to Be Me" is about Anna, a girl who also wants to be a dancer. Ask students what they must do to prepare for the work they want to do when they grow up.

English-
Language
Learner's
Book

Write the concept words on the board. Use them in sentences to illustrate their meanings.

- I want to be a **dancer** when I grow up because I like music.
- My **teacher** shows me how to do different dance moves.
- I want to study science so that I can be a **doctor** when I grow up.
- My parents are **worried** that I will not get good grades in science.
- I am **happy** when I dance because it makes me feel good.
- I am **unhappy** when I study science because I do not like it.

Concept Words
dancer
teacher
doctor
worried
happy
unhappy

Have students add these words to their Language Dictionaries

Directed Reading: "I Want to Be Me"

📖 **Summary** *Anna wants to be a dancer, but her parents want her to concentrate more on her studies. Anna decides to work hard at both.*

Use these sentences to walk students through the story.

Pages 2–5
- This is Anna. She loves to dance. She wants to be a ballet star someday.
- In the car, Anna tells her father about *The Nutcracker*.
- Anna's father is not happy because Anna did poorly on her math test.

Pages 6–9
- Anna is showing her father the book *Stories of the Great Ballets*.
- Anna's parents told her she could not perform in *The Nutcracker*.

❓ **QUESTIONS:**
pages 2–9
- Does Anna like to dance? (*yes*)
- What does Anna want to be when she grows up? (*a ballet dancer*)
- Why is Anna's father unhappy? (*Anna did poorly on her math test.*)

Pages 10–13
- Anna and her friend Maggie are at ballet class.
- Anna talks to Ms. Diaz about her problem.
- Anna's mother agrees to let Anna work hard at school and ballet.

Pages 14–16
- Here is Anna at her big show, *The Nutcracker*.
- Anna's parents are proud of her hard work.

❓ **QUESTIONS:**
pages 10–16
- Is Maggie Anna's best friend? (*yes*)
- What is the name of the ballet Anna performs in? (*The Nutcracker*)

(⭐ Focus Skill) ## Main Idea and Details

RETEACH Review the organizational pattern of *main idea* and *details* with students. Then draw on the board a two-column chart with the headings *Main Idea* and *Details*. Ask students to to complete the chart about "I Want to Be Me."

FLUENCY PRACTICE Ask students to read a paragraph from page 5 aloud. Have students use the illustration on page 7 to retell part of "I Want to Be Me" using as many vocabulary words and concept words as possible.

Interactive Writing: Comparison and Contrast Essay

PRETEACH Tell students that they are going to work with you to write an essay that compares and contrasts the jobs of a dancer and a doctor. Generate a Venn diagram with the circles labeled *Dancer* and *Doctor*. Have students work in small groups to brainstorm similarities and differences. Write their suggestions on the board.

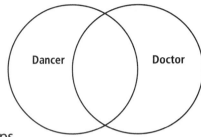

"Share the pen" with students by working with them to write the draft. Use these steps to think aloud the process:
- What are the similarities and differences?
- What are some details to support each point?
- Use the Venn diagram to help organize your ideas.

Encourage students to reread their sentences frequently to make sure they make sense and to help them plan what to write next.

Grammar: Main and Helping Verbs

PRETEACH Discuss the definitions of *main* verbs and *helping* verbs with students. Point out the following:
- A **verb** expresses action or a state of being.
- A **verb phrase** consists of a **main verb** preceded by at least one **helping verb**.
- The main verb is the most important verb in a verb phrase.
- A helping verb can work with the main verb to tell about an action.

Write the following sentences on the board and read them aloud:
- *I would be a good teacher because I am patient.*
- *I am studying English.*
- *I had been thinking about being a doctor.*

Tell students that the three sentences have verb phrases. *Be*, *studying*, and *thinking* are the *main* verbs; they are preceded by the *helping* verbs *would*, *am*, and *had been*.

Point out that sometimes the parts of a verb phrase are interrupted by words such as *not* or *never*, from other parts of speech.

Read the following sentences aloud. Ask students to identify the verbs. Then have them explain whether they are main verbs or helping verbs.
 I. Anna's mother was sitting at her desk. (*was, helping ; sitting, main*)
 2. Anna talked about her plans. (*talked, main*)
 3. Anna's parents worried about her plans. (*worried, main*)
 4. Anna was not doing well in school. (*was, helping ; doing, main*)
 5. Anna will study harder. (*will, helping ; study, main*)

FLUENCY PRACTICE Have volunteers read aloud the comparison and contrast essay that they completed in the writing activity.

Interactive Writing: Comparison and Contrast Essay

RETEACH Display the completed essay from Preteach. Read it aloud with students. Ask them what they would change about it and why. Discuss students' suggestions for changing or adding to the paragraph. Write the revised essay based on students' suggestions. Then have students copy the revised essay into their Language Journals.

Grammar-Writing Connection

RETEACH Write these sentences on the board and read them aloud with students:

Evelyn Cisneros went to New York to study dance.

Anna will study hard at school and take dance lessons.

Have volunteers identify the main and helping verbs in each sentence. Remind them that the *helping* verb precedes the *main* verb in a verb phrase. Then have students discuss with partners what they would like to be when they grow up, as well things they will need to do to prepare for their career choices. After sharing with partners, have students write several sentences describing their future career plans. Have students underline the verb phrase in each of their sentences. Check students' writing and suggest any corrections they need to make.

FLUENCY PRACTICE Have students read aloud the sentences they completed in the grammar activity.

Name _____

Fill in the blank in the sentence below to tell what you would like to be. Then write a few sentences about what you would do in that profession. Draw a picture below the sentences to show what you would do in that profession.

I would like to be a _____ when I grow up.

_____

_____

_____

TO THE TEACHER Ask students what they would like to be when they grow up. You might want to show students the names of different professions such as a lawyer, a policeman, an actor, a writer, a salesperson, and so on. Have students read their sentences aloud for sense.

Evelyn Cisneros: Prima Ballerina/I Want to Be Me • **Lesson 20** **121**

© Harcourt

Use with "Off and Running"

BEFORE

Building Background and Vocabulary

Build Background/Access Prior Knowledge

Have students look at the illustration on *Pupil Edition* page 502. Point to the girl and the woman. Tell students that both the woman and the girl would like to win an election. Then ask **Would you like to be president of your class? What would you do to win the election?** Record students' responses in a list like the one shown.

What I Would Do to Win the Election
visit my classmates at their residences
call my classmates on the phone
make campaign posters

Selection Vocabulary

PRETEACH Display Teaching Transparency 199 and read the words aloud. Then point to the pictures as you read the following sentences:

1. The woman is organizing a **campaign** to win the election. She is making posters and talking to the voters so that she can win.
2. The woman is talking to a voter at his **residence**. She is speaking with him at the place where he lives.
3. The voter wants to **endorse** the woman. He wants to tell others that he thinks she should win the election.
4. The other candidate has written **graffiti** on the wall of the building.
5. The graffiti is **obnoxious**. It is offensive. It damages a public building.

AFTER

Building Background and Vocabulary

Selection Vocabulary

RETEACH Revisit Teaching Transparency 199. Read the words aloud with students. Have students discuss the meanings of the words and answer questions such as: *Does* **obnoxious** *mean "pleasant" or "unpleasant"?*

Write these sentence frames on the board. Read each one aloud and ask students to choose a vocabulary word to complete it. Write students' responses in the blanks.

1. We will remove the _____ that someone wrote on the wall. (*graffiti*)
2. Sandra has lived at the same _____ all of her life. (*residence*)
3. I am upset when my friend does something _____. (*obnoxious*)
4. Tomás, a candidate for president, is organizing a _____. (*campaign*)
5. Many voters like Tomás's ideas and will _____ him in the election. (*endorse*)

Have students write the selection vocabulary words in their Language Dictionaries.

FLUENCY PRACTICE Encourage students to describe the illustrations on Teaching Transparency 199 by using the vocabulary words and any other words they know.

Build Background: "Off and Running"

Revisit the illustration on *Pupil Edition* page 502. Tell students that the girl is Miata and the woman is Doña Carmen. Explain that they have participated in different elections. Discuss with students what someone might do to win an election. (*organize a campaign, share ideas, call or visit friends*)

DISTANT VOYAGES

 ## Compare and Contrast

PRETEACH Tell students that authors often use a compare-and-contrast text structure to show how people, objects, or ideas are alike or different. Explain that the story compares and contrasts Miata and Doña Carmen. Draw a Venn diagram on the board. In the area where the circles intersect write: *Both wanted to win an election.* Tell students that this is one way in which Miata and Doña Carmen are alike. After students have read the story, work with them to complete the Venn diagram with examples from the text that compare and contrast the characters.

Directed Reading: "Off and Running"

RETEACH Use these sentences to walk students through the story.

- This is Miata. She is in the fifth grade.
- She is running for class president against a boy named Rudy.
- Miata calls her friends on the phone and asks for their votes.
- This is Miata's dad. Miata asks him if he knows anyone important.

- This is Miata's mom. She knows Doña Carmen, a woman who was once mayor of a town in Mexico.
- Miata wants to talk to the woman. Miata goes to visit the former mayor.

QUESTIONS:
pages 492–499

- Is Miata running for office? (*yes*) What office is it? (*class president*)
- How does Miata encourage her friends to vote for her? (*She calls them on the phone.*)

Pages 500-503

- This is the house of Doña Carmen.
- Miata comes to visit. She is carrying a loaf of bread as a gift.
- Doña Carmen greets Miata at the door.
- She tells Miata that she ran against her husband to become mayor.

Pages 504-506

- Doña Carmen speaks about what she focused on as mayor—education.
- Doña Carmen asks Miata what she is promising to do as class president.
- Miata says she wants to help make the school look pretty.
- Doña Carmen helps Miata with her promise by giving Miata flowers.

QUESTIONS:
pages 500–506

- Does Miata go to see the former mayor? (*yes*)
- In what place was Doña Carmen a mayor? (*a Mexican town*)
- What does Doña Carmen offer to do for Miata? (*She offers to help her with one of her campaign promises.*)

FLUENCY PRACTICE Ask a volunteer to read aloud a paragraph from *Pupil Edition* page 503.

Build Background: "Holidays, Family, and Fun"

PRETEACH Remind students that "Off and Running" is about Miata, a girl who is running for class president. In "Holidays, Family, and Fun," they will read about holidays that honor important American presidents. Like Miata, these men shared ideas about how to make things better.

English-
Language
Learners
Book

Write the concept words on the board and use them in sentences to illustrate their meanings.

Concept Words
celebration
parade
sharing
cards
picnics

- My city has a **celebration** with music and food on Memorial Day.
- On Independence Day, sometimes people march in a **parade**.
- We like **sharing** our special customs with other people on holidays.
- I send **cards** to my family and friends on Valentine's Day.
- We have **picnics** in the park when it is warm enough to eat outside.

Have students add the concept words to their Language Dictionaries.

Directed Reading: "Holidays, Family, and Fun"

Summary *People from all over the world have brought their customs to America. We celebrate these traditions on different holidays.*

Use these sentences to walk students through the story.

Pages 2–5
- This story is called "Holidays, Family, and Fun."
- Here are families from different countries. They have just arrived in America.
- This family is celebrating the Chinese New Year.
- Dr. Martin Luther King, Jr. worked so that people would be treated fairly.

Pages 6-9
- Here is José Martí. He believed that people should be treated equally.
- Here is George Washington, America's first President. This is Abraham Lincoln, the President who freed the slaves. We honor these men on Presidents' Day.
- On Valentine's Day some people give cards to one another they care.

QUESTIONS: pages 2–9
- Who was America's first President? (*George Washington*)
- What might you give someone on Valentine's Day? (*cards, candy, flowers*)

Pages 10–13
- These people are giving books to children. They are celebrating a holiday called Día de los Libros/ Día de los Niños, Day for Books/ Day for Children.
- Some states have Spanish names. Latino culture is important in America.
- On Memorial Day Americans honor soldiers who fought in wars.

Pages 14–16
- The day the United States won its freedom is Independence Day.
- This family is eating Thanksgiving dinner.

QUESTIONS: pages 10–16
- What do Americans celebrate on Independence Day? (*their freedom*)
- Who do we honor on Memorial Day? (*soldiers who fought in wars*)

(Focus Skill) Compare and Contrast

Review the compare-and-contrast text structure with students. Then draw a Venn diagram on the board. Ask students to revisit the story to find details to compare and contrast Presidents' Day and Independence Day. Use the information students find to complete the diagram.

> **FLUENCY PRACTICE** Ask students to read aloud page 9 from "Holidays, Family, and Fun."

Interactive Writing: Research Report

PRETEACH Tell students that they are going to work with you to write a research report that explains to a newcomer how to celebrate an American holiday. Explain that a research report includes an introduction, a body, and a conclusion. Show students how to use an inverted pyramid to narrow their choice of research topics to one specific topic that can be handled in a short report. Then have students brainstorm topics for a research report. Write their suggestions on the board.

"Share the pen" with students by working with them to write sentences for the research report. Use these steps to think aloud the process:

- Use the information from "Holidays, Family, and Fun" to organize your ideas.
- What information do I have about the holiday?
- What do people do on the holiday to celebrate it?

As students suggest sentences, write them on the board. Encourage them to reread the sentences to make sure they make sense. Using students' suggestions, write a draft of the report on the board.

Grammar: Action and Linking Verbs

PRETEACH Point out to students the following information about action and linking verbs:

- An **action verb** tells what the subject of a sentence did, does, or will do.
- A **linking verb** connects the subject of a sentence to a noun, a pronoun, or an adjective in the predicate that renames or describes the subject.
- The most common linking verbs are forms of *be: am, is, are, was, were.*

Write the following sentences on the board, and read them aloud:

- *Miata calls her friends on the phone.*
- *Miata visits Doña Carmen.*
- *Doña Carmen was a mayor.*

Tell students that in the first two sentences *calls* and *visits* are action verbs. Point out that an action verb is often followed by a direct object, a noun or pronoun that receives the action. The direct objects in the examples are *friends* and *Doña Carmen.* In the third sentence *was* is a linking verb.

Read the following sentences aloud. Ask students to identify each verb as an action or a linking verb.

1. Independence Day is a holiday in the United States. (*linking*)
2. Families share food on Thanksgiving Day. (*action*)
3. People celebrate holidays in different ways. (*action*)
4. George Washington was an American president. (*linking*)

FLUENCY PRACTICE Have volunteers read aloud the draft of the research report that they completed in the writing activity.

Interactive Writing: Research Report

RETEACH Display the draft of the report from the Preteach activity. Read it aloud with students. Ask them what revisions they would make to it. Discuss students' suggestions for changes or additions to the report. Write the revised report based on students' suggestions. Then have students copy the revised report into their Language Journals.

Grammar-Writing Connection

RETEACH Write these sentences on the board and read them aloud with students:

- *Thanksgiving is my favorite holiday.*
- *I share food with my family on that special day.*

Ask volunteers to point out the action verb and the linking verb in the sentences. Have students work in pairs or in small groups to discuss what their favorite holiday is and why. Then have students draw a picture to show their ideas. Encourage students to describe each pictures aloud. Then work with them to write a sentence or two that describes their picture. Remind students that an action verb tells what the subject of a sentence did, does, or will do and that a linking verb connects the subject of a sentence to a noun, a pronoun, or an adjective in the predicate that renames or describes the subject. Check students' writing, and suggest any corrections they need to make.

FLUENCY PRACTICE Have students choose a paragraph from "Holidays, Family, and Fun" to read aloud.

Name _____

A In the space below, draw a picture for the outside of a Valentine's Day card for a friend or family member.

B Write a message for the inside of your card. Tell your friend or family member how much you care about him or her.

_____

_____

_____

_____

TO THE TEACHER Model sample messages to include in the card and the expression "Happy Valentine's Day!" Have students read their messages aloud for sense.

© Harcourt

LESSON 22

Use with "Little by Little"

BEFORE

Building
Background
and Vocabulary

Build Background/Access Prior Knowledge

Have students look at the illustrations on *Pupil Edition* pages 514–515. Point to the girl standing by the teacher and explain that it is the girl's first day in a new school. Then ask students to share their experiences about going to a new school or a new place. Ask: **How does going to a new school make you feel? Why does it make you feel this way?** Record students' responses in a chart like this one.

Going to a new school makes me feel	because
worried	I might not be popular
nervous	people might think I'm funny and laugh at me
tired	I will be very busy with homework

Selection Vocabulary

PRETEACH Display Teaching Transparency 208 and read the words aloud. Then point to the pictures as you read the following sentences:

1. The boy is sick with **polio**. It is a disease that causes paralysis.
2. The boy is suffering from **immobility**. He is unable to move.
3. The girl feels **dismay** because she missed the bus. She is disappointed that the bus left without her.
4. Bugs are **despised** by many people. They are disliked by many people.
5. I cannot **decipher** what these writings say. I am unable to read and understand the writings.
6. The girl is **astonished** that she has a birthday party. She did not know she was going to have a party. She is surprised.

AFTER

Building
Background
and Vocabulary

Selection Vocabulary

RETEACH Revisit Teaching Transparency 208. Read the words aloud with students. Have students discuss the meanings of the words and answer questions such as: *Does* **despised** *mean "liked" or "disliked?"*

Write the following sentence frames on the board. Read each sentence and ask students to choose a vocabulary word to complete it. Write students' responses in the blanks.

1. My sister feels _____ because she has not made any friends. (*dismay*)
2. I could not _____ the man's handwriting. (*decipher*)
3. My grandmother got sick with _____ when she was a girl. (*polio*)
4. My parents were _____ by my good grades. (*astonished*)
5. Ana _____ vegetables when she was a girl, so she refused to eat them. (*despised*)
6. I had to stay in bed when I hurt my leg because of the _____. (*immobility*)

Have students write these words in their Language Dictionaries.

FLUENCY PRACTICE Have students read the completed sentence frames aloud.

Build Background: "Little by Little"

Revisit the pictures on *Pupil Edition* pages 514–515. Tell students that the girl is Jean Little. Explain that Jean wants to fit in on her first day in fifth grade. Have students recall how they felt on their first day of school.

DISTANT
VOYAGES

Author's Purpose and Perspective

PRETEACH Tell students that Jean Little is the author as well as the main character in the story. Explain that the story is told from Jean's perspective, or point of view. Point out that students can complete a character chart to help them understand an author's purpose and perspective. Draw a three-column chart on the board with the headings *Actions*, *Motive*, and *Appearance*. Tell students that Jean wanted to fit in with her classmates. After students read the story, have them revisit it to find details that show Jean's point of view about fitting in. Record students' findings in the appropriate columns in the chart. After the chart is completed, ask students what the author's purpose was for writing the story? Ask: **Was it to entertain, to persuade, or to inform?**

Directed Reading: "Little by Little"

RETEACH Use these sentences to walk students through the story.

Pages 514–517

- This is Miss Marr's fifth-grade class.
- This is Jean. She is telling this story.
- Jean's eyes are crossed. It is hard for her to read numbers and letters.
- Jean must sit close to the chalkboard in order to read it.

Pages 518–519

- It is recess. The children are on the playground.
- This blond girl is Shirley Russell. Jean wishes Shirley would be her friend.
- Shirley is mean to Jean.

QUESTIONS: pages 514–519

- Is Jean blind? (*no*)
- Which grade is Jean in? (*fifth*)
- Why does Jean need to sit near the chalkboard? (*She has trouble seeing what is written on it.*)

Pages 520–521

- Jean has no one to play with at recess. She feels lonely.
- She leans against this tree for comfort.

Pages 522–526

- Miss Marr reads aloud a math test. Jean has trouble with multiplication.
- She waits to write down the answers until Miss Marr reads them aloud.
- Then she checks each answer. The popular girls see that Jean is cheating.
- Jean feels badly. She goes to Miss Marr to confess what she did.
- Miss Marr forgives Jean, and Jean promises never to cheat again.

QUESTIONS: pages 520–526

- Does Jean take a math test? (*yes*)
- How does Jean feel at recess? (lonely)
- What does Jean do to make herself feel better about cheating on the test? (*She confesses what she did to her teacher and promises never to do it again.*)

FLUENCY PRACTICE Ask a volunteer to read a paragraph from *Pupil Edition* page 520 aloud.

Build Background: "The Hamster from Room 24 Is Missing"

PRETEACH Remind students that "Little by Little" is about Jean, a girl who feels lonely on her first day in a new school. In "The Hamster from Room 24 Is Missing" they will read about students in a fifth-grade class. Like Jean, they are worried about a problem that they have.

Concept Words
popular
mystery
bored
snacks

Write the concept words on the board and use them in sentences to illustrate their meanings.

- I want to be **popular** in school so that I have a lot of friends.
- Where is my book? It is a **mystery** what happened to it.
- I feel **bored** in math class because it is too easy.
- My father put some candy, pretzels, and other **snacks** in my lunch bag.

Have students add these words to their Language Dictionaries.

Directed Reading: "The Hamster from Room 24 Is Missing"

Summary *Herman is the class hamster, and he is missing. Mrs. Parker and her class look for Herman on the baseball field, but they can't find him. Finally, they find him—snacking on nuts in another classroom!*

Use these bulleted sentences to walk students through the story.

Pages 2–5
- This is Herman. He's the class hamster. This is Mrs. Parker, the teacher.
- Alex is going to feed Herman.
- The door to Herman's cage is open, and the cage is empty.
- Everyone is shocked when Alex tells them that Herman is missing.

Pages 6–9
- Now Mrs. Parker and her class are in the gym. They are looking for Herman.
- Some students think Herman could be on the balance beam, doing cartwheels on the mat, or jumping on the trampoline.

QUESTIONS:
pages 2–9
- Is Herman the teacher? (*no*)
- Who is going to feed Herman? (*Alex*)

Pages: 10–16
- This is Kim. She thinks Herman went to look for food.
- Mrs. Parker leads her class on a search at the baseball field.
- Mr. Hom found Herman in his classroom. Herman was eating nuts.
- Alex carefully carries Herman back to his cage. Everyone is happy.

QUESTIONS:
pages 10–16
- Does the class find Herman? (*yes*)
- What was Herman eating? (*nuts*)

RETEACH Review the concepts of author's purpose and perspective. Explain that from the author's perspective the story character Alex is *very* knowledgeable about hamsters and is determined to find Herman. Tell students to revisit the story to find details about Alex's actions, motive, and appearance that support this perspective.

FLUENCY PRACTICE Ask students to read a paragraph from page 14 aloud.

Interactive Writing: Outline

PRETEACH Tell students that they are going to work with you to write an outline for a story about a problem they had at school. Explain that an outline can help them organize information in time order. Have students work in small groups to brainstorm a main idea and supporting details for the story. Have them write their details on notecards.

Show students how to use an outline format. Point out that main ideas are headed with Roman numerals and supporting details are headed with capital letters, numbers, and lower case letters. Show students how to punctuate an outline properly and how to align letters with letters and numbers with numbers.

"Share the pen" with students by working with them to write a story outline on the board. Using students' suggestions from the note cards, help them write main ideas. Elicit from students suggestions for supporting details. After the outline is complete, have students review it to make sure that the information is listed in correct time order.

Grammar: Present Tense

PRETEACH Point out the following:

- The **tense** of a verb tells the time of an action. There are three basic verb tenses: present, past, and future. A present-tense verb shows that the action is happening now or happens over and over.
- The form of a present-tense verb changes to agree with the subject of the sentence. This is called subject-verb agreement.

Write the following sentences on the board and read them aloud:

- *Jean wishes Shirley would be her friend.*
- *Jean feels lonely.*
- *The popular girls talk to Jean.*

Tell students that in the first two sentences *Jean* is the subject and the present-tense verbs *wishes* and *feels* agree with *Jean*. In the third sentence, *girls* is the subject and the present-tense verb *talk* agrees with *girls*.

Write the following sentences on the board. Ask students to select the correct verb to show present tense. Have them say the whole sentence.

1. The hamster (like/likes) to eat snacks. (*likes*)
2. The students (look/looks) for the hamster. (*look*)
3. Mrs. Parker (help/helps) the students. (*helps*)
4. Do you (like/likes) hamsters? (*like*)

FLUENCY PRACTICE Have volunteers read aloud the completed outline from the writing activity.

Interactive Writing: Outline

RETEACH Display the completed outline from the Preteach activity. Read it aloud with students. Ask them what revisions they would make to it. Discuss students' suggestions for changes or additions to the outline. Write the revised outline based on students' suggestions. Then have students copy the revised outline into their Language Journals.

Grammar-Writing Connection

RETEACH Write these sentences on the board and read them aloud with students:

- *Jean feels lonely at her new school.*
- *The fifth-grade students look for the missing hamster.*

Ask volunteers to identify the present tense verbs in the sentences. (*feels*, *look*) Then, have students work in pairs or in small groups to discuss a problem they now have in school. Ask students to draw pictures to show their ideas. Encourage students to describe their pictures aloud. Then work with them to write a sentence or two describing their pictures. Remind students that the form of a present-tense verb changes to agree with the subject of the sentence. Check students' writing and suggest any corrections they need to make.

FLUENCY PRACTICE Have students use the illustration on page 3 to retell part of "The Hamster from Room 24 is Missing." Encourage them to use as many vocabulary words and concept words as possible.

Imagine four other places where the hamster from "The Hamster from Room 24 Is Missing" might be. Draw pictures to show where the hamster might be. Below each drawing write a sentence about the picture.

_____

_____

_____

_____

© Harcourt

TO THE TEACHER Before students begin drawing, have students generate a list of places where a hamster might be hiding. Write the list on the board.

Use with "Dear Mr. Henshaw"

Build Background/Access Prior Knowledge

Have students look at the illustrations on *Pupil Edition* pages 536–537. Point to the boy and tell students that he is writing in his diary. Then ask: **Do you write in a diary? How often do you write in a diary? What do you write about in your diary?** Record their responses in a list like this one.

In my diary I write about
problems I have.
ideas I have.
my family and friends.

Selection Vocabulary

PRETEACH Display Teaching Transparency 217, and read the words aloud. Then point to the pictures as you read the following sentences:

1. A boy **submitted** his picture to the teacher. He presented it to her.
2. The boy drew a sugar **refinery**. It is where raw sugar is made fine.
3. The road to the refinery has a steep **grade**. You have to climb a high slope to get to the refinery.
4. The thick wall will **muffle** the sound of the dog's barking. It will make the sound harder to hear.
5. The wall will muffle the dog's barking because it is **insulated**. The wall is surrounded by material that keeps sound from leaking out.
6. A **partition** separates the dog from the cat. It keeps them apart.
7. The cat **prowls** outside of the wall. It roams around quietly and slyly.

Selection Vocabulary

RETEACH Revisit Teaching Transparency 217. Read the words aloud with students. Have students discuss the meanings of the words and answer questions such as: *Is a* **grade** *sloping or flat*?

Write the following sentence frames on the board. Read each one aloud and ask students to choose a vocabulary word to complete it. Write students' responses in the blanks.

1. A _____ separates our class and the first-grade class. (*partition*)
2. The room should be _____ so that it is less noisy. (*insulated*)
3. I _____ a story to my teacher. (*submitted*)
4. My class visited the _____ where raw sugar is made fine. (*refinery*)
5. I am scared when an animal _____ outside of the house. (*prowls*)
6. I will not be able to hear you. The door will _____ the sound. (*muffle*)
7. The _____ of this hill is so steep that he has to change his bike's gears. (*grade*)

Have students write the words in their Language Dictionaries.

> **FLUENCY PRACTICE** Have students read the completed sentence frames aloud.

Build Background: "Dear Mr. Henshaw"

Revisit the pictures on *Pupil Edition* pages 536–537. Tell students that the boy is Leigh. Explain that Leigh is writing in his diary about some new problems that he has. Discuss with students what someone might do if he or she has a problem. (*look for a way to fix it, ask family for help, talk with friends*)

DISTANT VOYAGES

Focus Skill   Compare and Contrast

PRETEACH Remind students that authors sometimes organize text in a way that compares and contrasts story elements. Explain that this organization helps readers understand the relationships between people, places, objects, ideas, and events. Draw a Venn diagram on the board with the headings *Leigh's problems at home* and *Leigh's problems at school* in each circle. Tell students that one of Leigh's problems at school is that he needs to write a story for the Young Writers' Yearbook. Write that information in the appropriate circle. After students finish the story, have them revisit it to find other examples of Leigh's problems at home and school. Record students' findings on the diagram.

Directed Reading: "Dear Mr. Henshaw"

RETEACH Use these sentences to walk students through the story.

Pages 536–539
- This is Leigh Botts. He is writing in his diary.
- In his diary, Leigh writes about some problems he has.
- Someone at school is stealing Leigh's lunch.
- He is having trouble thinking what to write for a writing contest.
- Leigh decides to invent a lunchbox alarm to catch the lunch thief.

Pages 540–545
- Leigh works on the alarm in his room. He gets his alarm to work.
- Leigh's alarm goes off at school.
- Leigh doesn't catch the thief, but he feels like a hero.
- Leigh's dad calls. Leigh misses his dad.

? QUESTIONS: pages 536–545
- Does Leigh write in his diary? (*yes*)
- What does Leigh build to stop the lunch thief? (*an alarm*)
- How does Leigh feel after his alarm goes off at school? (*He feels like a hero.*)

Pages 546–549
- Leigh remembers when they took a trip in his dad's big truck.
- Leigh decides to write about the trip for the Yearbook contest.
- He writes about how the truck was full of grapes and how his father kept the heavy truck on the curvy roads.

Pages 550–554
- Leigh's story wins Honorable Mention. He is invited to meet a famous author.
- Leigh goes with other students to meet the famous author.
- The author calls Leigh an author and tells him she liked his story.

? QUESTIONS: pages 546–554
- What did Leigh write about for the contest? (*a trip he took with his father*)
- Did Leigh meet a famous author? (*yes*)
- What did the famous author call Leigh? (*an author*)

FLUENCY PRACTICE Ask a volunteer to read a paragraph from *Pupil Edition* page 541 aloud.

Build Background: "The Potluck Picnic"

PRETEACH Remind students that "Dear Mr. Henshaw" is about Leigh, a boy who writes in his diary about some problems he has. In "The Potluck Picnic" they will read about Troy, a boy who also writes about a problem he has.

*English-
Language
Learners
Book*

Concept Words
potluck
dish
dessert
cookbook
taste

Write these words on the board and use them in sentences to illustrate their meanings.

- Each student will bring food so that we can have a **potluck** picnic.
- Vegetable soup is my favorite **dish**. I like ice cream for **dessert**.
- I learned how to cook chicken from a **cookbook**.
- I will **taste** a little bit of the rice to see if I like it.

Have students add the concept words to their Language Dictionaries.

Directed Reading: "The Potluck Picnic"

Summary *Troy's class is having a potluck picnic. Ms. Daily and Maggie help Troy make a family dish for the picnic. Troy calls his invention the Sammy sandwich after his new baby brother.*

Use these bulleted sentences to walk students through the story.

Pages 2–5
- Ms. Sanchez is telling her students to bring a dish their family enjoys to a potluck picnic. This is Troy. He is writing in his class diary.
- Troy is trying to think of what he will bring to the potluck picnic.
- Troy is saying that he is cooking his own invention for the picnic.

Pages 6–9
- Maggie gives Troy a hug. Then they sit at the table talking to Ms. Daily.
- Ms. Daily is at the house. Troy's mother is having a baby.

**QUESTIONS:
pages 2–9**
- What does Ms. Sanchez ask everyone in the class to bring to the picnic? (*a favorite family dish*)
- Who gives Troy a hug? (*Maggie*)
- Why are Troy's parents at the hospital? (*Troy's mother is having a baby.*)

Pages 10–13
- Ms. Daily and Maggie help Troy make a special dish for the picnic.
- Troy's invention has his family's favorite food: waffles from his mother; ham from his father; mashed sweet potatoes from his sister; raisins from Troy.

Pages 14–16
- Troy has written the recipe for his special invention in his class diary.
- Troy and his sister are on the phone. They are talking to their father. He is telling them they have a new baby brother named Sammy.
- At the potluck picnic, Troy's class likes his invention, the 'Sammy sandwich.'

**QUESTIONS:
pages 10–16**
- What does Troy write in his diary? (*He writes the recipe for his invention.*)
- Does Troy have a new baby sister? (*no*)

⭐Focus Skill Compare and Contrast

RETEACH Review the concept of compare and contrast with students. Then draw a Venn diagram on the board with the headings *Leigh's Problems* and *Troy's Problems* in each circle. Ask students to revisit the stories in this lesson to find details that illustrate how the characters, Leigh and Troy, are alike and different. Record students' findings on the diagram.

> **FLUENCY PRACTICE** Ask students to read aloud Troy's journal entry on page 13.

Independent Writing: Diary Entry

PRETEACH Tell students that they are going write a diary entry about an imaginary problem. Point out that a diary entry begins with a date, and it is written from the first-person perspective.

Have students work in small groups to generate ideas for the diary entry. Put a sample concept web for Troy's diary entry on the board. Then have each student complete a concept web for the diary entry. Suggest that students use their concept webs to organize their ideas in a way that makes sense. Have students complete the activity by writing a draft of a diary entry.

something I make with Ms. Daily

What I should bring to the potluck picnic

make a new dish

all of my family's favorite foods

Grammar: Past and Future Tenses

PRETEACH Discuss the definition of past and future tense verbs with students. Point out the following:

- A verb in the **past tense** shows that the action happened in the past. Form the past tense of most verbs by adding *-ed*.
- A verb in the **future tense** shows that the action will happen in the future. To form the future tense of a verb, use the helping verb *will*.

Write the following sentences on the board and read them aloud:

- *Leigh missed his dad.*
- *Leigh helped his friend Barry.*
- *Leigh will be a famous author.*

Tell students that in the first two sentences the verbs *missed* and *helped* are in the past tense. In the third sentence *will be* is in the future tense.

Point out that to form the past tense of verbs that end in a vowel plus a consonant (except *y*), double the consonant before adding *-ed*. For example, the past tense of the verb *stop* is *stopped*.

Write the following sentences on the board. Ask students to say whether the verb in each sentence is in the past or in the future tense.

1. Troy will prepare a special dish. (*future*)
2. Ms. Sanchez asked the students to write in their diaries. (*past*)
3. The students talked about the picnic. (*past*)
4. The students will taste Troy's dish. (*future*)
5. Troy walked home. (*past*)

FLUENCY PRACTICE Have volunteers read aloud the diary entry that they drafted in the writing activity.

Independent Writing: Diary Entry

RETEACH Have volunteers read their diary entries from the Preteach activity aloud. Ask them what changes they would make to them and why. Discuss students' suggestions for changes or additions. Have students make the revisions. Then have students copy the revised diary entry into their Language Journals.

Grammar-Writing Connection

RETEACH Write these sentences on the board and read them aloud with students:

- *Troy wanted to make a special dish.*
- *He will use a cookbook to get ideas.*

Ask volunteers to underline the past and future tense verbs in the sentences on the board. (*wanted*, past; *will use*, future)Then, have students work in pairs or in small groups to discuss something that happened to them in the past and something that they will do in the future. Ask students to draw a picture to show their ideas. Encourage students to describe their pictures aloud. Then work with them to write a sentence or two that describes each picture. Remind students that a past tense verb shows that the action happened in the past and a future tense verb shows that the action will happen in the future. Check students' writing and suggest any corrections they need to make.

FLUENCY PRACTICE Have students use the illustration on pages 10–11 to retell part of "The Potluck Picnic." Encourage them to use as many vocabulary words and concept words as possible.

Name _____

Cut out these words and periods. Use them to make as many sentences as you can.
You may use a card to make more than one sentence.

I	dish	a	wonderful
tasted	will	My teacher	needed
to	cookbook	liked	dessert
my friend	It	my	the
use	make	favorite	find
.	.	.	.

TO THE TEACHER Ask pairs of students to form sentences from the cards. Remind students that they can reuse a card to make another sentence. You may want to model forming a sentence such as *I tasted my favorite dish*. Have students say aloud their sentences for sense. Then have them write their sentences in their Language Journals.

© Harcourt

Use with "**Frindle**"

Build Background/Access Prior Knowledge

Have students look at the illustrations on *Pupil Edition* pages 568–569. Point to the boy raising his hand and tell students that he is learning where words come from. Ask students to share their experiences with unfamiliar words. Ask: **Did you ever not know what a word means? What do you do if you do not know the meaning of a word?** Record their responses in a list on the board.

Selection Vocabulary

PRETEACH Display Teaching Transparency 226 and read the words aloud. Then point to the pictures as you read the following sentences:

1. The girl is **beaming** because she is happy. She is smiling very warmly.
2. The girl has a **reputation** for being a good student. Other people think she always gets good grades.
3. The TV will **sidetrack** the boy. The TV will keep him from doing the homework he needs to do.
4. The boy is so **absorbed** by the story that he does not notice the ice-cream truck. The story attracts his attention completely.
5. The children are walking down the **aisle** of the movie theater. The aisle separates groups of seats into different sections.
6. The president takes an **oath** before taking office. He asks God to watch that he is being honest.

Selection Vocabulary

RETEACH Revisit Teaching Transparency 226. Read the words aloud. Have students work in pairs to discuss the meanings of the words and to answer questions such as: *Does* **beaming** *mean "smiling" or "crying"?*

Write the following sentence frames on the board. Read each one and ask students to choose a vocabulary word to complete it. Write students' responses in the blanks.

1. If you talk on the phone while you study, it will _____ you. (*sidetrack*)
2. After the movie, I walked up the _____ to leave the theater. (*aisle*)
3. If you cheat on a test, you will get a bad _____. (*reputation*)
4. Luisa was so _____ in writing a poem that she did not see me. (*absorbed*)
5. We were _____ when we won the contest. (*beaming*)
6. The new president took an _____ before he started his job. (*oath*)

Have students write the selection vocabulary words in their Language Dictionaries.

FLUENCY PRACTICE Have students read the completed sentence frames aloud.

Build Background: "Frindle"

Revisit the pictures on *Pupil Edition* pages 568–569. Tell students that the boy is Nick, and he is learning how people agree on what words mean. Have students ways to find the meaning of a word. (*dictionary, context, ask someone*)

DISTANT
VOYAGES

Author's Purpose and Perspective

PRETEACH Tell students that good readers look for clues in a story that will help them to determine the author's purpose and perspective. Explain that they can use a character chart to help them organize story details that will reveal the author's purpose and perspective. Draw a three-column chart on the board with the headings *Actions*, *Motive*, and *Appearance*. Tell students that Nick is known for his many ideas. Write that information under the second heading. Once students have read the story, have them revisit it to find details to complete the chart.

Directed Reading: "Frindle"

RETEACH Use these sentences to walk students through the story.

Pages 566–569

- This is Nick Allen. He's in the fifth grade.
- Nick is known in school for his many ideas.
- This is Nick's teacher, Mrs. Granger.
- Nick asks who decides that a word means what it means.
- Mrs. Granger says, "You, me, and everyone."
- She says we decide what goes in the dictionary.

QUESTIONS:
pages 566–569

- Is Nick sneezing in class? (*no*)
- What does Nick want to ask his teacher? (*how words get their meanings*)
- Who does Mrs. Granger say gives words their meanings? (*She says we give words their meanings.*)

Pages 570–571

- Nick is walking home from school with his classmate Janet.
- They are both walking on the curb, trying to keep their balance.
- Janet finds a pen near the curb.

Pages 572–574

- Nick begins calling a pen a frindle.
- This is the saleslady at the store. Nick asks her for a frindle.
- The lady doesn't know what the word means, so Nick points to a pen.
- Nick sends his friends to the store to buy frindles.
- Nick and his friends take an oath to use only the word *frindle* when talking about a pen.

QUESTIONS:
pages 570–574

- Does Nick buy a frindle at the store? (*yes*)
- Who does Nick send to buy more frindles? (*his friends*)
- What does Nick do in the story to help the saleslady know what he wants? (*He points to the pens on the shelf.*)

FLUENCY PRACTICE Ask a volunteer to read a paragraph from *Pupil Edition* page 569 aloud.

Concept Words
topic
computer
organized
dictionary
check out

Build Background: "Library, Library"

PRETEACH Remind students that "Frindle" is about Nick, a boy who asks many questions. In "Library, Library," they will read about a place to find answers to their questions.

Write the concept words on the board. Use them in sentences to illustrate their meanings.

- The **topic** of my report is art.
- The library has a **computer** to help me quickly find books.
- At the library books are **organized** on the shelves so that you can find them.
- A **dictionary** tells you the meaning of a word.
- I decided to **check out** library some books. Now I can take them home.

**English-
Language
Learners
Book**

Have students add the concept words to their Language Dictionaries.

Directed Reading: "Library, Library"

📖 **Summary** *Libraries have books that help with schoolwork and books that are read for fun.*

Use these bulleted sentences to walk students through the story.

Pages 2–5
- This is a library. Look at all of the books and magazines.
- This librarian is helping a student find a book.
- Another student is finding a book by using the library computer.
- This girl is using the card catalog to find a library book.

Pages 6–9
- This student is looking in an encyclopedia. Encyclopedias have information about many topics.
- These students are looking in a dictionary. To find definitions of words.
- Here is an atlas. It has maps and gives geographic information about places.

**❓ QUESTIONS:
pages 2–9**
- Can you use the library's computer to find a book? (*yes*)
- Which book has maps? (*atlas*)
- What is a dictionary? (*A book that gives the definitions of words.*)

Pages 10–13
- This girl is using a thesaurus. She is looking up a word in it to find other words with the same and the opposite meanings of her word.
- These nonfiction books give information about facts and real events.
- The table of contents of a book shows what information is in the book.
- Fiction books are about imaginary people, places, and things.

Pages 14–16
- These people are using their library cards to check out books.
- They will read the books at home and return them to the library.

**❓ QUESTIONS:
pages 10–16**
- Does a thesaurus have information about imaginary places in it? (*no*)
- What does a book's table of contents show? (*what is in the book*)
- What do people use to check books out of the library? (*library cards*)

(Focus Skill) Author's Purpose and Perspective

RETEACH Review the concept of author's purpose and perspective with students. Then write these sentences on the board: *"Library, Library" is written to inform. The author tells about the many sources of information one can find at a library*. Ask students to revisit the story to find examples that illustrate the author's purpose. List their findings beneath the sentences on the board.

FLUENCY PRACTICE Ask students to read page 2 of "Library, Library" aloud.

Independent Writing: Research Report, Outline

PRETEACH Tell students that they are going to work with you to write an outline for a research report about the meaning of a word. Review the structure of a research report: introduction, body, and conclusion. Have students work in small groups to brainstorm possible words to write about. Provide a dictionary for them to consult. Put a sample outline on the board. Then have each student complete an outline with more specific information for the research report.

I. **An unusual word**

   A. Why I don't know what it means

   B. Why it is unusual

II. **What the word means**

   A. What the dictionary says

   B. How people use it

III. **Conclusion of what I learned**

   A. Summary of word's meaning

   B. My reaction to it

Remind students to consult their outlines when they write their research reports in the next lesson.

Grammar: Principal Parts of Verbs

PRETEACH Point out the following to students:

- The **principal parts of a verb** are its four basic forms: the **infinitive**, the **present participle**, the **past**, and the **past participle**.
- Participles in verb phrases are forms used with helping verbs.

Write the following sentences on the board and read them aloud:

- *Nick likes to invent new words.*
- *Nick is learning about the dictionary.*
- *Nick has shared the words with his friends.*

Tells students that in the first sentence *invent* is an infinitive. In the second sentence *learning* is a present participle. In the third sentence *shared* is a past participle.

Write the following sentences on the board. Have students identify the verb in each one and tell which principal part of the main verb is used.

1. You have studied in the library. (*have studied; past participle*)
2. You are looking for information. (*are looking; present participle*)
3. Many people are using the library. (*are using; present participle*)
4. I have checked out a book. (*have checked out; past participle*)

FLUENCY PRACTICE Have volunteers read aloud portions of their outline that they completed in the writing activity.

Independent Writing: Research Report Outline

RETEACH Have volunteers display their outlines from the Preteach activity. Ask students what changes they would like to make to their outlines and why. Discuss students' suggestions for revisions. Have students make the revisions. Then have them copy the revised outlines into their Language Journals.

Tell students they will return to the outlines that they have written in the next writing lesson.

Grammar-Writing Connection

RETEACH Write these sentences on the board and read them aloud with students:

- *Many people have looked for information at the library.*
- *Now they are also using the computer to find information.*

Have students identify the principal parts of the verbs in the sentences on the board. Have students work in pairs or in small groups to discuss where they have found answers to their questions in the past and where they can find the answer to a question that they have right now. Then have students draw a picture to show their ideas. Encourage students to describe their pictures orally. Then work with them to write a sentence or two that describes each picture. Check students' writing and suggest any corrections they need to make.

FLUENCY PRACTICE Have students use the illustrations on page 6–7 to retell part of "Library, Library." Encourage them to use as many vocabulary words and concept words as possible.

Imagine that you want to let your friends know about the things they can find in a library. Draw a poster showing what a library is like. Then write a few sentences to use as labels for the poster, and include them in your drawing.

© Harcourt

TO THE TEACHER You may want to model with students some labels for their posters. Tell students that labels attract attention, make a poster more interesting, and provide more information.

Frindle/Library, Library • **Lesson 24**   **145**

Use with "The Fun They Had"

BEFORE

Building Background and Vocabulary

Build Background/Access Prior Knowledge

Have students look at the illustrations on *Pupil Edition* pages 586–587. Point to the boy and the girl holding the book and tell students that they are living in the future. Ask students what they think school might be like in the future. Then ask: **What do you think school will be like in the future? What is school like now?** Record their responses in a chart like the one shown.

School In the Future	School Now
will not have books	has books
will use discs	does not use many discs
there will be homework	there is homework

Selection Vocabulary

PRETEACH Display Teaching Transparency 234, and read the words aloud. Then point to the pictures as you read the following sentences:

1. Ann looked **sorrowfully** at her old house. She is sad that she is moving. She does not want to leave.
2. Ann's parents want to move, so she does not **dispute** them. She accepts their decision. She does not argue with them.
3. It is hard for Ann to become **adjusted** to a new school. Things are different and Ann will have to used to the differences.
4. Ann walked into class **nonchalantly**, but inside she was very nervous. She acted as if it wasn't important to her.
5. Ann told her parents **loftily** that she had a great day. She didn't let them know that she was nervous. She acted in a haughty manner.

AFTER

Building Background and Vocabulary

Selection Vocabulary

RETEACH Revisit Teaching Transparency 234. Read the words with students. Have students discuss the meanings of the words and answer questions such as: *Does* **dispute** *mean "to argue" or "not to argue"?*

Write the following sentence frames on the board. Read each one aloud, and ask students to choose a vocabulary word to complete it. Write students' responses in the blanks.

1. It took me a month to become _____ to my new school. *(adjusted)*
2. Timothy spoke _____ to the teacher when he told her he knew the answer. *(loftily)*
3. My best friend told me _____ that she was moving. *(sorrowfully)*
4. I sometimes _____ my parents when they tell me to do my homework. *(dispute)*
5. Sara opened the book _____ because she had no interest in it. *(nonchalantly)*

Have students write the selection vocabulary words in their Language Dictionaries.

FLUENCY PRACTICE Have students read the sentence frames aloud.

Build Background: "The Fun They Had"

Revisit the pictures on *Pupil Edition* pages 586–587. Tell students that the boy is Tommy and the girl is Margie. Explain that they are reading a book about school in the past. Discuss with students how school is now and how it might be the same or different in the future.

DISTANT
VOYAGES

 Draw Conclusions

PRETEACH Tell students that to understand a story, they must apply their own knowledge and experience while reading the information that the author gives. Explain that as we read, we draw conclusions from several sources. These include the words and actions of the characters and the information the author states directly. Draw a three-column chart on the board with the headings *Selection Information*, *Personal Knowledge and Experience*, and *Conclusion*. Tell students that in the future students will be taught by machines, not by people. Write this information under the first heading. Work with students to complete the chart after students have finished the story. Remind students that they can draw conclusions by combining what they know personally with what they have learned in a story. Ask students to conclude who will be teachers in the future.

AFTER

Reading "The Fun
They Had"

Pages 584–587

Pages 588–589

QUESTIONS:
pages 584–589

Pages 590–592

QUESTIONS:
pages 590–592

Directed Reading: "The Fun They Had"

RETEACH Use these sentences to walk students through the story.

- Tommy and Margie live in the future.
- They are reading a book about what schools used to be like.
- Margie is taught by a mechanical teacher.
- The mechanical teacher broke down, but a man came and fixed it.

- Margie reads the lessons on a screen.
- She puts her homework and tests in a slot in the machine.

- Do Tommy and Margie live in the future? (*yes*)
- What are they reading about in the book? (*what schools used to be like*)
- Who teaches Margie? (*a mechanical teacher*)

- This is a picture from the book Tommy and Margie are reading.
- It shows a human teacher and kids learning together in a classroom.
- There are books, papers, and homework on the desk.
- Margie thinks that this school looks like more fun than hers.

- Is this a picture of Margie's school? (*no*)
- Who is the teacher? (*a human, a man*)
- What does Margie think about schools in the old days? (*She thinks it looks like more fun than her school.*)

FLUENCY PRACTICE Ask a volunteer to read a paragraph from *Pupil Edition* page 589 aloud. Encourage students to describe the illustration on *Pupil Edition* 591. Have students use as many vocabulary words as they can in their descriptions.

Build Background: "School 2501"

PRETEACH Remind students that "The Fun They Had" is about, a girl and a boy who live in the future. In "School 2501," they will read about other children, who live in the future.

English-Language Learners Book

Write the concept words on the board. Use them in sentences to illustrate their meanings.

Concept Words
backpack
discs
jump rope
lunch
same

- I carry my books, pencils and homework to school in a **backpack.**
- We will use **discs** for the computer instead of books in the future.
- Many children like to play with a **jump rope** during recess.
- Students will always eat **lunch** when they are in school.
- Some things will not change in the future, so they will be the **same.**

Have students add the concept words to their Language Dictionaries.

Directed Reading: "School 2501"

Summary *Kira and Arthur are students who live in the future. Kira finds some things from the past and brings them to school. Kira and her friends find that schools from the past were similar to their school.*

Use these sentences to walk students through the story.

Pages 2–5
- Here are Arthur and Kira. They live in the future.
- At school, Arthur is looking inside Kira's backpack. Kira found things she wants to show to her class.

Pages 6–9
- Look at the school library. There are no books. All the information is on discs.
- This is Darren. He is Arthur and Kira's friend.
- This is Mr. Frank. He is the teacher. He is showing Kira's book to the class.
- Kira has other things in her backpack to show the class.

QUESTIONS: pages 2–9
- Do Arthur and Kira live in the past? *(no)*
- What is in the library instead of books? *(discs)*

Pages 10–13
- No one in Kira's class has ever seen a jump rope before.
- The students play rocketball and wear rocket packs that let them float.
- Kira, Arthur and Darren go to the library to find out what school was like in the past.

Pages 14–16
- Kira, Arthur and Darren are looking at a picture of a school from the past.
- The school from the past they see looks different. But then they realize that school itself was like their school. It had classrooms, teachers and tests.
- Kira and her friends also realized that students from the past were very similar to students of the future.

QUESTIONS: pages 10–16
- Has the class ever seen a jump rope before? *(no)*
- Why do the friends go to the library? *(to find out about schools in the past)*

 (Focus Skill) **Draw Conclusions**

Review with students how to draw conclusions. Write this sentence from the selection on the board: *I wonder if they had discs in their library.* Call on a volunteer to read it aloud. Then ask students to use their personal knowledge to draw a conclusion about discs and books. (*They both provide people with information.*)

> **FLUENCY PRACTICE** Ask students to read page 3 from "School 2501" aloud.

Independent Writing: Research Reports Edit

`PRETEACH` Tell students to use the outline they wrote in Lesson 24 to write a draft for a research report about the meaning of a word. Remind students that all writers spend a good deal of time revising and polishing their first drafts. Explain that in this lesson students will revise and proofread the drafts they completed. Have students work together in pairs to edit their research reports. Write the following questions on the board to help them think aloud the editing process:

- *Do I use facts and examples to develop major points?*
- *Does my writing have a logical organization? Is anything confusing or unnecessary?*
- *Are my sentences well constructed?*
- *Do I have any mistakes in spelling, punctuation, or capitalization?*

Suggest that students revise their research reports using the questions they answered to think aloud the editing process.

Grammar: Regular and Irregular Verbs

`PRETEACH` Discuss the definitions of a regular and an irregular verb with students. Point out the following:

- **Regular verbs** are verbs that end with *-ed* in the past tense.
- An **irregular verb** is a verb that does not end with *-ed* in the past tense. Irregular verbs have special spellings for the past tense and past participle.

Write the following sentences on the board and read them aloud:

- *Margie's computer broke down.*
- *Margie and Tommy read a book about schools.*
- *Margie thought that school in the past was more fun.*

Tell students that the verbs *broke, read, thought,* and *was* are irregular verbs. They are in the past tense and do not end with *-ed.*

Write the following sentences on the board. Ask students to say what the verb is and tell whether it is regular or an irregular verb.

1. Kira jumped with the rope. *(jumped;* regular*)*
2. The students read about schools in the past. *(read;* irregular*)*
3. The teacher asked for the jump rope. *(asked;* regular*)*
4. Kira thought about many things. *(thought;* irregular*)*
5. She returned the book to the library. *(returned;* regular*)*

FLUENCY PRACTICE Have volunteers read aloud the research report that they edited in the writing activity.

Independent Writing: Research Report, Edit

RETEACH Have volunteers read their research reports from the Preteach activity aloud. Ask students what changes they made in their revisions and why they made them. Then have students copy the revised research report into their Language Journals.

Grammar-Writing Connection

RETEACH Write these sentences on the board and read them aloud with students:

- *Margie thought schools in the past were more fun than hers.*
- *Kira read that schools in the past were similar to hers.*

Ask students to identify the irregular verbs in the sentences on the board. (*thought, were, read, were*) Then have students work in pairs or in small groups to discuss what they think schools were like in the past. Ask students to draw a picture to show their ideas. Encourage students to describe their pictures aloud. Then work with them to write a sentence or two that describes each picture. Remind students that irregular verbs in the past tense do not end with *-ed*. Check students' writing and suggest any corrections they need to make.

FLUENCY PRACTICE Have students choose a page from "School 2501" to read aloud. Have students use illustrations on pages 4–5 to retell part of "School 2501." Encourage them to use as many vocabulary words and concept words as possible.

Name _____

Imagine that you are going to create a time capsule so that you can tell students in the future what your school was like. Draw a map of your school. Then write a few sentences to label the map, explaining what you do in each different part of the school. Write your sentences in your Language Journal.

© Harcourt

TO THE TEACHER You may want to model some labels, checking to make sure that students are using irregular verbs correctly. You may also want to use a shoebox for a time capsule and put the completed maps in it. You can then have the students imagine they are in the future and have them open the time capsule to look at and read the labels on the maps.

Use with **"Across the Wide Dark Sea"**

Build Background/Access Prior Knowledge

Have students look at the illustrations on *Pupil Edition* pages 604–605. Point to the boy with his father and tell students that they are going on a trip to someplace new. Ask: **How does going on a trip to a new place make you feel? Why do you feel this way?** Record their responses in a chart like this:

I feel	because
excited	I might like it.
afraid	something bad might happen.
nervous	I don't know what it will be like.

Selection Vocabulary

PRETEACH Display Teaching Transparency 244 and read the words aloud. Then point to the pictures as you read the following sentences:

1. The people see the **vast** ocean. It is very large.
2. The people are **huddled** together. They are crowded together.
3. Another man **lurked** behind the barrels. He is hidden behind the barrels. The people cannot see him.
4. The people live in a **settlement.** They have created a colony.
5. The houses are made of **beams.** Long pieces of wood are used to make the frames of the houses.
6. The crew must furl the ship's sails. They roll and fasten the sails.
7. This ship's **rigging** organizes the sails and other equipment that help the ship to move.

Selection Vocabulary

RETEACH Revisit Teaching Transparency 244. Have students work in pairs to discuss the meanings of the words and to answer questions such as: Does **huddled** mean *crowded together* or *separated*?

Write the following sentence frames on the board. Read each sentence and ask students to choose a vocabulary word to complete it. Write students' responses in the blanks.

1. I _____ close to my parents because I was afraid. *(huddled)*
2. I did not see my brother when he _____ behind a tree. *(lurked)*
3. The crew must _____ the ship's sails after the trip. *(furl)*
4. The ship's _____ is not working, so the ship will not move. *(rigging)*
5. The people built a _____ so that they would have a place to live. *(settlement)*
6. My grandfather built his house with _____. *(beams)*
7. The land was so _____ that there was space for many houses. *(vast)*

Have students write these words in their Language Dictionaries.

FLUENCY PRACTICE Have students read the sentence frames aloud. Encourage them to describe the illustrations on Teaching Transparency 244 using the vocabulary words and any other words they know.

BEFORE

**Reading
"Across the Wide
Dark Sea"**
pages 602–617

Build Background: "Across the Wide Dark Sea"

Revisit the pictures on *Pupil Edition* pages 602–603. Tell students that the boy is going on a journey in a ship. Discuss with students how someone might feel about going to a new place (*afraid, excited, nervous*).

**DISTANT
VOYAGES**

 Connotation / Denotation

PRETEACH Tell students that words can have the same basic meaning yet still suggest differences. Explain that the denotation of a word is its dictionary definition. Many words have more than one denotation; for example, the word *trip*. Connotation refers to additional feelings and ideas that the word suggests. A word may have positive or negative connotations.

AFTER

**Reading
"Across the Wide,
Dark Sea"**

Pages 602–605

Pages 606–607

Pages 608–609

♩ QUESTIONS:
pages 602–609

Pages 610–613

Pages 614–615

Pages 616–617

♩ QUESTIONS:
pages 610–617

Directed Reading : "Across the Wide Dark Sea"

RETEACH Use these sentences to walk students through the story.

- People sailed across the sea many years ago on the Mayflower.
- This boy is telling the story. This is his father.
- They are sailing from England.

- The people on the ship live below deck.
- It is very crowded and uncomfortable.

- Some days the sky is blue and the winds fill the sails.
- Other days it is stormy and rough.

- Are the people sailing across the ocean? *(yes)*
- What do they sail in? *(a ship)*
- What are the living conditions like below deck? *(They are crowded and uncomfortable.)*

- The boy stands on deck after the storm has passed.
- The storm pulls a man overboard. Here he is holding onto a rope.
- One of the storms damages the ship. Point to the crack in the beam.
- The people use tools on the boat to fix it.
- The ship sails on for many weeks.
- At last the sailors spot land.
- Here they are dropping the anchor.
- A small group of people goes ashore to see if it is safe.

- On land, women wash the dirty clothes.
- The people find a place to make their new home.

- Does a man fall overboard? *(yes)*
- What do the women wash when they finally reach land? *(the dirty clothes)*

FLUENCY PRACTICE Ask a volunteer to read a paragraph from page 605 aloud. Encourage students to describe the illustrations on *Pupil Edition* 606–607. Encourage students to use as many vocabulary words as they can in their descriptions.

Build Background: "Food for Fun"

PRETEACH Tell students that in "Food for Fun," they will read about a boy who is going to new places with his aunt. Ask students what they like to do on trips.

English-
Language
Learners
Book

Write these words on the board. Use them in sentences to illustrate their meanings.

Concept Words
excited
restaurant
invited
flavor
ordered
menu

- I am **excited** because I am very happy that my aunt is coming to visit me.
- We are going to eat in a **restaurant** that has Mexican food.
- My aunt **invited** me to go with her to the restaurant.
- The food tasted great. It has a wonderful **flavor**!
- I **ordered** tacos at the restaurant.
- The **menu** listed many different kinds of Mexican food.

Have students add these words to their Language Dictionaries.

Directed Reading : "Food for Fun"

📖 **Summary** *A boy is excited because his Aunt Cara is coming to visit. She invites him to go with her to restaurants that have food from many different countries. She writes restaurant reviews.*

Pages 2–3
- The boy telling the story got a letter from his Aunt Cara.
- Aunt Cara writes restaurant reviews for a newspaper in Florida.
- She is coming to California to write some restaurant reviews.

Pages 4–7
- Last summer the boy visited his Aunt Cara in Florida.
- Aunt Cara is arriving at the airport in California.
- She asks the boy to choose a slip of paper to decide what they will eat first.

QUESTIONS: pages 2–7
- Is the boy excited? *(yes)*
- Who is coming to visit him? *(his Aunt Cara)*

Pages 8–15
- The boy and Aunt Cara go to a Mexican restaurant for lunch.
- The boy orders avocado soup and Aunt Cara orders vegetable fajitas.
- They go to an American restaurant for dinner and eat meatloaf and salmon.
- Next they go to an Italian restaurant and order linguine and fettuccine.
- They also go to an Indian restaurant and order curried chicken and eggplant.

Page 16
- Aunt Cara will send the boy a copy of her restaurant reviews when they are printed in the newspaper.

QUESTIONS: pages 8–16
- Do the boy and Aunt Cara go to a Chinese restaurant? *(no)*
- What does the boy order in the American restaurant? *(meatloaf)*

★ Focus Skill Connotation/Denotation

Review the definitions of connotation and denotation with students. Then draw a two-column chart on the board with the headings **Positive** and **Negative.** Ask students to revisit the story to complete the chart using the connotations of words from the story.

FLUENCY PRACTICE Ask students to read page 3 aloud. Then have students use the illustration on page 5 to retell part of "Food for Fun." Encourage them to use as many vocabulary words and concept words as possible.

Interactive Writing: Rhymed Poem

PRETEACH Tell students that they are going to work with you to write a rhymed one-stanza poem about a trip to someplace new. Generate a concept web. Have students work in small groups to pick a phrase for the center circle and brainstorm images and sensory words and phrases to write in the surrounding circles of the web.

exciting

flavors

A trip to a Mexican restaurant

spicy food

"Share the pen" with students by working with them to write the draft. Use these steps to think aloud the process:

- *How can I start my poem?*
- *What images and feelings do I want in the stanza? How can I arrange them in lines?*
- *What rhyme scheme will work best? (abab, aabb, or abcb)*
- *What words can I choose or change to fit the rhythm and rhyme scheme?*

As you work with students to help them revise the poem, have them read lines aloud to evaluate the effect of images and word choices.

Grammar: Perfect Tenses

PRETEACH Discuss the definitions of perfect verb tenses with students. Point out the following:

- A verb in the **present perfect tense** shows that the action started to happen sometime before now and is not yet finished.
- A verb in the **past perfect tense** shows that the action happened before a specific time in the past.
- A verb in the **future perfect tense** shows that the action will have happened before a specific time in the future.

Point out that each of the three perfect tenses uses the past participle of the verb with a form of the helping verb *have*. The form of the helping verb shows the tense.

Write the following sentences on the board. Ask students to identify the perfect tense of each verb.

1. The boy had visited Aunt Cara in Florida. *(past perfect)*
2. The boy has had some fun times with his aunt. *(present perfect)*
3. The boy had eaten tacos before. *(past perfect)*
4. The boy will have visited other restaurants when the newspaper prints the reviews. *(future perfect)*
5. Aunt Cara has worked for a newspaper. *(present perfect.)*

FLUENCY PRACTICE Have volunteers read aloud the poem that they completed in the writing activity.

Interactive Writing: Rhymed Poem

RETEACH Read the rhymed poem aloud. Ask students what they would change about it and why. Discuss students' suggestions for changing or adding to the poem. Revise the poem. Then have students copy the revised poem into their Language Journals.

Grammar-Writing Connection

RETEACH Write these sentences on the board and read them aloud with students:

The boy has never visited an Indian restaurant.
He had visited an Italian restaurant.

Ask students to underline twice the perfect-tense verbs in the above sentences. Have students work in pairs or in a small group to discuss new places that they have or have not visited. Then have students draw a picture to show their ideas. Encourage students to describe their pictures aloud. Work with students to write a sentence or two that describes their picture. Remind them that the form of the helping verb shows the tense. Check students' writing and suggest any corrections they need to make.

FLUENCY PRACTICE Have students share their drawings and read aloud the sentences that describe them.

Name _____

Imagine that you are going to open your own restaurant. You would like to serve your favorite foods. Design a menu below for your restaurant. First, write a list of the dishes. Then, write a short description of each dish. Finally, include a price for each dish. You can also make some drawings to decorate your menu.

TO THE TEACHER You may want to put a model menu on the board so that students can see the format. Explain that the descriptions often include sensory images and are designed to sell the food. When students finish the menus, they can work in pairs to practice ordering from them.

Across the Wide Dark Sea/Food For Fun • **Lesson 26** **157**

Use with "Name This American"

Build Background/Access Prior Knowledge

Have students look at the illustrations on *Pupil Edition* pages 628–629. Point to the people and tell students that they are characters in a play. Ask students to share their experiences with plays. Ask: **Have you ever been to a play? What are some things needed to do a play?** Record their responses in a list like the one at the right.

Things needed to do a play
director
costumes
actors

Selection Vocabulary

PRETEACH Display Teaching Transparency 253 and read the words aloud. Then point to the pictures as you read the following sentences:

1. The **distinguished** singers are on the stage. They are famous singers.
2. The singers are singing an **anthem**. It is a song of praise.
3. A man listening needs an **interpreter** to tell him what the song means.
4. The women are **indebted** to the woman in the picture.
5. The woman in the picture fought for women's **suffrage**. She wanted women to have the right to vote.
6. The car salesman **stumps** the buyer. He confuses him.
7. The salesman is **misleading** the car buyer. He is leading him to the wrong conclusion.
8. The car buyer wants a **guarantee**. He wants a promise.

Selection Vocabulary

RETEACH Revisit Teaching Transparency 253. Have students work in pairs to discuss the meanings of the words and to answer questions such as: Does **distinguished** mean *famous* or *unknown*?

Write the following sentence frames on the board. Read each sentence and ask students to choose a vocabulary word to complete it. Write students' responses in the blanks.

1. Sara does not speak English, so she needs an _____. *(interpreter)*
2. We sing the national _____ before we play baseball. *(anthem)*
3. I am lost because the map _____ me. *(stumps)*
4. We are _____ to Mrs. Parson for her help. *(indebted)*
5. We had a ceremony in honor of a _____ politician. *(distinguished)*
6. The new car has a _____. *(guarantee)*
7. We studied the women's _____ movement, which fought for the right to vote. *(suffrage)*
8. My friend is _____ me with silly clues. *(misleading)*

Have students write these words in their Language Dictionaries.

FLUENCY PRACTICE Have students read the sentence frames aloud. Encourage them to describe the illustrations on Teaching Transparency 253 using the vocabulary words and any other words they know.

Build Background: "Name This American"

Revisit the pictures on *Pupil Edition* pages 628–629. Tell students that the people are characters in a play about important Americans. Point to the people on the right and explain that they are trying to guess who the man on the left is. Discuss with students how they would prepare to do a play *(find a director, get costumes, choose actors)*.

DISTANT
VOYAGES

Cause and Effect

PRETEACH Tell students that an **effect** is what happens because of some action or event. The **cause** is the reason it happens. Draw a two-column chart on the board with the headings *Causes* and *Effects*. Tell students that a woman was an interpreter and guide. Write this information in the chart in the **Causes** column. Complete the chart after students finish the story.

Directed Reading: "Name this American"

RETEACH Use these bulleted sentences to walk students through the story.

Pages 626–629

- Uncle Sam is in a play about a quiz program.
- These are the panelists. They are trying to identify mystery guests.
- The mystery guests are famous Americans.
- Walter Hunt invented the safety pin.

Pages 630–631

- The panelists correctly identify Gutzon Borglum, who sculpted Mt. Rushmore.

Pages 632–633

- The panelists cannot identify Dolley Madison, the wife of President James Madison.
- She saved a picture of George Washington before the White House was burned by the British.

 QUESTIONS:
pages 626–633

- Is this a play about a quiz program? *(yes)*
- What did Gutzon Borglum sculpt? *(Mt. Rushmore)*

Pages 634–635

- The panelists identify Sacajawea, an Indian guide and interpreter.
- She helped the explorers Lewis and Clark.

Pages 636–637

- The panelists also identify Babe Ruth, a famous baseball player.

Pages 638–639

- The quiz program ends.
- The program and the play honor these famous Americans.
- Can you identify these famous Americans?

QUESTIONS:
pages 634–639

- Was Sacajawea an interpreter? *(yes)*
- Who was Babe Ruth? *(a baseball player)*
- What do the quiz program and the play do? *(They honor famous Americans.)*

FLUENCY PRACTICE Ask volunteers to read lines from page 635 aloud. Encourage students to describe the illustration on *Pupil Edition* 632–633. Ask students to use as many vocabulary words as they can in their descriptions.

Build Background: "Let's Do a Play"

BEFORE

Making Connections
pages 644–645

PRETEACH Remind students that "Name This American" is a play about famous Americans. Tell students that in "Let's Do a Play," they will read about how to put on a play. Discuss with students the different kinds of things that must be done to put on a play.

English-Language Learners Book

Write these words on the board and use them in sentences to illustrate their meanings.

Concept Words
perfume
costumes
choose
director
auditorium
rehearsing

- My school will **perform** a play about American holidays.
- We need to sew **costumes** for the actors to wear during the play.
- Our teacher will **choose** who will be the actors in the play.
- The **director** will help us practice for the play.
- Our parents will sit in the **auditorium** to watch us do the play.
- We spent many weeks **rehearsing** to prepare to do the play.

Have students add these words to their Language Dictionaries.

Directed Reading: "Let's Do a Play"

AFTER

Skill Review
pages 646–647

📖 **Summary** *It takes a lot of work to put on a play. The actors rehearse with the director. Other people make costumes or paint scenery. The stagehands carry the props and scenery around the stage.*

Pages 2–5
- These are the actors who will perform the actions on the stage.
- This is the director who is in charge of the play.
- You also have to make costumes to do a play.
- Costumes make the play look more real.

Pages 6–7
- Props are the things on stage that the actors use.
- The scenery shows where the play takes place.
- People called stagehands carry the props and scenery on and off the stage.

❓ QUESTIONS: pages 2–7
- Are the actors in charge of a play? *(no)*
- What are the things that the actors use on stage? *(props)*

Pages 8–15
- An auditorium is where people sit when they watch a play.
- A stage is where the actors perform the play.
- Here you have a closer look at the stage.
- Everyone needs to practice so they will do well.

Page 16
- Everyone in a play must work together.
- If everybody works hard, the audience will like the play.

❓ QUESTIONS: pages 8–16
- Do people sit in an auditorium to watch a play? *(yes)*
- What do the actors do the night before a show? *(They practice.)*

⭐(Focus Skill) Cause and Effect

Remind students of the definitions of cause and effect. Refer back to the chart of causes and effects on the board. Ask students to look through the story "Let's Do a Play" for examples of cause and effect.

> **FLUENCY PRACTICE** Ask students to read page 7 aloud. Have students use the illustration on page 2 to retell part of "Let's Do a Play." Encourage them to use as many vocabulary words and concept words as possible.

Independent Writing: Story Introduction

PRETEACH Tell students that they are going to write the beginning of a story about a famous person or character that they admire. Have students work in small groups to brainstorm famous persons to write about. Work with students to plan using these steps:

1. Decide on a famous person or character.
2. Decide on a problem for him or her to solve.
3. Decide on a setting.
4. Plan a beginning that introduces the character, the setting, and the problem.

Have students write a draft. Tell them to reread frequently to check that it makes sense. Encourage them to use descriptive words and phrases.

Grammar: Contractions and Negatives

PRETEACH Discuss the definition of a contraction with students. Point out the following:

- A **contraction** is the shortened form of two words put together to form one word.
- An **apostrophe** takes the place of one or more letters that are left out.
- Subject pronouns are often used with verbs in contractions, as in *she'll.*

Write the following sentences on the board and read them aloud:

- *The panelists didn't identify Dolley Madison.*
- *The panelists couldn't name all of the famous Americans.*
- *They've had fun during the quiz program.*

Tell students that in the first two sentences the contraction contains the word *not. Not* is a negative often used in contractions. In the third sentence, the contraction is formed with the pronoun *they,* which refers to the panelists, and the helping verb *have.*

- Point out that only one negative is used in a sentence.
- Also tell students to avoid contractions in formal writing such as reports.

Read the following questions aloud. Ask students to answer the first three questions using a negative and a contraction. Then ask them to answer the last two questions, using a contraction:

1. Have you acted in a play? *(No, I haven't.)*
2. Did the actors learn their lines? *(No, they didn't.)*
3. Can you do a play without actors? *(No, you can't.)*
4. What will the stagehands do? *(They'll move the props.)*
5. Who are the actors? *(Answers may vary: They're the actors; He's the actor; I'm the actor.)*

FLUENCY PRACTICE Have volunteers read aloud the introduction that they completed in the writing activity.

Independent Writing: Story Introduction

RETEACH Have volunteers read aloud their introductions. Use these questions to help them think aloud how to revise:

- **Does my introduction have a famous person or character?**
- **Does my introduction have a problem for the character to solve?**
- **Does my introduction use descriptive words and phrases?**

Have students revise their introductions by adding descriptive words and phrases. You may also want students to complete their story by adding a body with events that try to solve the problem and an ending that tells the solution. Then have them copy the revised story into their Language Journals.

Grammar-Writing Connection

RETEACH Write these sentences on the board and read them aloud with students:

Who are Dolley Madison and Babe Ruth?
They're famous Americans.

Ask students to identify the contraction in the sentences above. Have students work in pairs or in small groups to talk about a famous person and discuss what that person has done. Then have students draw a picture to show their ideas. Encourage students to describe their pictures orally. Then work with them to write a sentence or two containing contractions that describe their picture. Remind students that an apostrophe takes the place of one or more letters that are left out in a contraction. Check students' writing and suggest any corrections they need to make.

FLUENCY PRACTICE Have volunteers read aloud the story that they completed in the writing activity.

Name _____

You are going to draw and label a stage. Revisit pages 10–11 of "Let's Do a Play" to help you with your drawing.

© Harcourt

TO THE TEACHER Have students draw a picture of a stage. Have them use as many of the selection words and concept words as possible to label their drawing. you may want students to color their drawings and display them in the classroom.

LESSON 28

Use with "What's the Big Idea, Ben Franklin?"

Build Background/Access Prior Knowledge

Have students look at the illustrations on *Pupil Edition* pages 650–651. Point to the man flying the kite and tell students that his name is Benjamin Franklin. Ask students to share what they know about Franklin. Ask: **Do you know who Benjamin Franklin is? Why is he an important man?** Record their responses in a list like this:

Benjamin Franklin
had many ideas.
lived in America around the time of its independence.
experimented with electricity.

Selection Vocabulary

PRETEACH Display Teaching Transparency 262 and read the words aloud. Then point to the pictures as you read the following sentences:

1. The two men are signing a **treaty** or an agreement.
2. One of the men is wearing a uniform that shows his **honors**.
3. A woman is holding the new **edition** of her book.
4. A man is using a **contraption** to record the men for television.
5. A flag is **suspended** behind the men and woman.
6. Our country will never cancel or **repeal** the law against stealing.

Selection Vocabulary

RETEACH Revisit Teaching Transparency 262. Read the words with students. Have students work in pairs to discuss the meanings of the words and to answer questions such as: Does **repeal** mean *cancel* or *not to cancel*? Does **edition** mean *many books* or *one book*?

Write the following sentence frames on the board. Read each sentence and ask students to choose a vocabulary word to complete it. Write students' responses in the blanks.

1. We _____ a flag from the house to decorate for Independence Day. *(suspended)*
2. The United States and England signed a _____ to end the war. *(treaty)*
3. Do you think the government will _____ the law? *(repeal)*
4. David checked the most recent _____ of the dictionary. *(edition)*
5. My father used a _____ to fix the car. *(contraption)*
6. The soldier received many _____ after the battle. *(honors)*

Have students write these words in their Language Dictionaries.

FLUENCY PRACTICE Have students read the sentence frames aloud. Encourage them to describe the illustrations on Teaching Transparency 262 using the vocabulary words and any other words they know.

BEFORE

Reading
"What's the Big
Idea, Ben
Franklin?"
pages 650–667

Build Background: "What's the Big Idea, Ben Franklin?"

Revisit the pictures on *Pupil Edition* pages 650–651. Tell students that Benjamin Franklin lived in the United States around the time of the Declaration of Independence. Explain that Franklin had lots of great ideas to make life better. Discuss with students some of his ideas *(electricity, inventions)*. Ask students if they have ever invented anything.

DISTANT
VOYAGES

★ Focus Skill — Connotation/Denotation

PRETEACH Tell students that words can suggest feelings or ideas. Explain that the **denotation** of a word is its dictionary definition and that **connotation** refers to additional feelings and ideas that a word suggests. A word may have positive or negative connotations. Draw a two-column chart on the board with the headings **Positive** and **Negative**. Have students help you complete the chart with descriptions of Ben Franklin after they read the story.

AFTER

Reading
"What's the Big
Idea, Ben
Franklin?"

Directed Reading : "What's the Big Idea, Ben Franklin?"

RETEACH Use these bulleted sentences to walk students through the story.

Pages 650–653

- Ben Franklin had many big ideas.
- Ben Franklin was an inventor.
- He put together an almanac.

Pages 654–657

- Ben Franklin thought lightning and electricity were the same.
- Ben became very famous because of his big ideas about electricity.
- He also improved the mail delivery system.

🔎 **Questions:**
pages 650–657

- Was Ben Franklin an inventor? *(yes)*
- What did Ben have a lot of? *(big ideas)*

Pages 658–661

- In 1757, Ben Franklin was sent to London.
- Ben tried to help keep England and America friendly.

Pages 662–663

- Ben went to France to get support for the United States.
- At 79, Ben returned to the United States.
- Everyone was excited to see him.
- This is his daughter Sarah. She was so excited she fell into a wheelbarrow.

🔎 **Questions:**
pages 658–665

- Did Ben live in Russia for a while? *(no)*
- Why did Ben go to France? *(He wanted to get support for the United States.)*

FLUENCY PRACTICE Ask a volunteer to read a paragraph from page 653 aloud. Encourage students to describe the illustrations on *Pupil Edition* 655. Ask students to use as many vocabulary words as they can in their descriptions.

Build Background: "Lights Out!"

PRETEACH Remind students that "What's the Big Idea, Ben Franklin?" is about Ben Franklin, a famous American inventor. Tell students that in "Lights Out!" they will read more about Ben Franklin.

English-
Language
Learner's
Book

Write these words on the board and use them in sentences to illustrate their meanings.

Concept Words
inventions
heat
electricity
lightning
machine

- New **inventions** help solve problems.
- In the winter, we need **heat** to keep our house warm.
- Televisions and computers run on **electricity.**
- I saw **lightning** and heard thunder during the rainstorm.
- The mechanic used a **machine** to fix the car.

Have students add these words to their Language Dictionaries.

Directed Reading: "Lights Out!"

📖 **Summary** *Ben Franklin held many jobs. He is probably most famous for the things he invented.*
Use these bulleted sentences to walk students through the story.

Pages 2–5
- Ben Franklin worked for many years as a printer and a publisher.
- He is probably most famous for his inventions.
- Franklin thought of a better and safer way to warm a home.

Pages 6–7
- Many people did not know about electricity and lightning.
- Ben decided to prove that lightning was caused by electricity.

❓ **QUESTIONS:**
pages 2–7
- Did Ben Franklin work as a printer and a publisher? *(yes)*
- What did Franklin invent to heat people's homes? *(a stove)*

Pages 8–9
- Ben proved that lightning is electricity.

Pages 10–13
- Ben invented the lightning rod.

- Franklin was the head of all the post offices in the country.
- Franklin invented an odometer to keeps track of how many miles are traveled.

Pages 14–16
- Franklin invented an instrument that played music with drinking glasses.
- Franklin made a new kind of eyeglasses.
- Ben Franklin wanted to share his ideas with everyone

❓ **QUESTIONS:**
pages 8–16
- Did Franklin prove that electricity caused lightning? *(yes)*
- What did Franklin invent to make buildings safer during lightning storms? *(the lightning rod)*

(Focus Skill) Connotation/Denotation

Review the definitions of connotation and denotation. Then draw on the board a two-column chart with the headings **Positive** and **Negative.** Complete the chart with the connotations of descriptive words from the story.

FLUENCY PRACTICE Ask students to read page 13 aloud. Then, have students use the illustrations on pages 8–9 to retell part of "Lights Out!" Encourage them to use as many vocabulary words and concept words as possible.

Interactive Writing: Play

PRETEACH Tell students that they are going to work with you to write a scene in a play based on an event in the life of Benjamin Franklin. Generate a concept web. In the center circle write the phrase *An event in the life of Benjamin Franklin.* In one of the surrounding circles, write the phrase: *how he proved his ideas about electricity and lightning.* Have students work in pairs or groups to write in the surrounding circles additional events that could be acted out.

how he proved his ideas about electricity and lightning

An event in the life of Benjamin Franklin

"Share the pen" with students to write a script for the play. To guide the writing process, write the following terms on the board and help students review the elements and structure of a play:

- *cast of characters (a list of the characters' names)*
- *setting (the time and place)*
- *stage directions (sentences, in parentheses, that tell the actors what to do)*
- *dialogue (the words characters speak)*

Grammar: Adverbs

PRETEACH Discuss the definition of an adverb with students. Point out the following:

- An *adverb* is a word that describes a verb, an adjective, or another adverb.
- An adverb tells how, when, where, or to what extent. Many adverbs that tell how end in *-ly.*

Write the following sentences on the board and read them aloud:

- *Benjamin Franklin became very famous.*
- *He carefully studied electricity.*
- *His test with the kite worked well.*

Tell students that in the first sentence the adverb *very* describes the adjective *famous.* In the second sentence, the adverb *carefully* describes' the verb *studied.* In the third sentence the adverb *well* describes the verb *work.* Point out that *well* is an adverb, unless it means "healthy." *Good* is an adjective.

Write the following sentences on the board. Ask students to identify the adverb and the word that it describes:

1. Benjamin Franklin quickly developed new ideas. *(quickly; developed)*
2. His ideas soon became famous. *(soon; became)*
3. We use his inventions today. *(today; use)*
4. Franklin often thought about electricity. *(often; thought)*
5. Working with electricity can be very dangerous. *(very; dangerous)*

FLUENCY PRACTICE Have volunteers read lines from the play that they completed in the writing activity.

Interactive Writing: Play

RETEACH Display the completed play from Preteach. Read it aloud with students. Ask them what they would like to change about it and why. Discuss students' suggestions for changing to or adding to the play. Write the revised play based on students' suggestions. Then have students copy the revised play into their Language Journal.

Invite students to take turns acting the play. You may want to encourage students to write additional scenes based on the life of Benjamin Franklin.

Grammar-Writing Connection

RETEACH Write these sentences on the board and read them aloud with students:

Benjamin Franklin is a very famous inventor.
He worked hard to make life better.

Ask volunteers to identify the adverbs in the above sentences.
Then, have students work in pairs or in a small group to discuss Franklin's contributions to his country. Suggest students draw a picture to show one of Franklin's contributions. Encourage students to describe their pictures aloud. Then work with them to write a sentence or two with adverbs that describe their picture. Remind students that an adverb describes a verb, an adjective, or another adverb. Check students' writing and suggest any corrections they need to make.

FLUENCY PRACTICE Have students describes their pictures aloud to the class.

Name _____

Write the names of four things we use electricity for today. Draw a picture of each thing.

1. _____ 2. _____

3. _____ 4. _____

© Harcourt

TO THE TEACHER Read aloud the directions with students. You may want to brainstorm a list of electronic devices with them. Encourage students to explain their drawings aloud.

LESSON 29

Use with "Lewis and Clark"

BEFORE

Building
Background
and Vocabulary

Build Background/Access Prior Knowledge

Have students look at the illustrations on *Pupil Edition* pages 678–679.
Point to the explorers and tell students that they are travelling across the
country. Ask students why the men
could be travelling. Then ask students
to share their experiences with travel.
Ask: **Why could these men be
travelling? Do you travel? Why do you
travel?** Record their responses in two
lists like this one:

The men are traveling because	I travel
they want to explore new land.	to see interesting sights.
they want to find a place to live.	to have fun.
it is their job.	to spend time with my family.

Selection Vocabulary

PRETEACH Display Teaching Transparency 271 and read the words aloud.
Then point to the pictures as you read the following sentences:

1. It is raining **profusely**. It is raining very heavily. It is pouring.
2. The sky looks **dismal**. It is gray and cloudy. It looks gloomy.
3. The man is in **peril**. He might fall. He is in danger.
4. The two men are experiencing an **ordeal**. They are having a difficult
   experience.
5. The **terrain** is rocky. The land is rocky.
6. These people are receiving an award because they are held in high
   esteem. They are very respected.

AFTER

Building
Background
and Vocabulary

Selection Vocabulary

RETEACH Revisit Teaching Transparency 271. Read the words with
students. Have students work in pairs to discuss the meanings of the
words and to answer questions such as: Does **dismal** mean *cheerful* or
gloomy? Does **profusely** mean *heavily* or *lightly*?

Write the following sentence frames on the board. Read each sentence
and ask students to choose a vocabulary word to complete it. Write
students' responses in the blanks.

1. My mother and I had a terrible _____ when our car broke down.
   (*ordeal*)
2. We gave our teacher a gift to show our _____ for her. (*esteem*)
3. The _____ is very flat. (*terrain*)
4. If you're not careful, your life could be in _____ . (*peril*)
5. Tina was so grateful that she thanked me _____ . (*profusely*)
6. It was a rainy and _____ day. (*dismal*)

Have students write these words in their Language Dictionaries.

FLUENCY PRACTICE Have students read the sentence frames aloud.
Encourage them to describe the illustrations on Teaching Transparency 271 using
the vocabulary words and any other words they know.

Build Background: "Lewis and Clark"

Revisit the pictures on *Pupil Edition* pages 678–679. Tell students that the explorers are Lewis and Clark. Explain that President Jefferson sent Lewis and Clark to explore new territory that went to the Pacific Ocean. Discuss with students what the explorers might find on their trip (*animals, people, sights*). Create a list of student responses on the board.

DISTANT VOYAGES

Focus Skill) Cause and Effect

PRETEACH Tell students the reason something happens is the cause. The things that happen are the effects. Authors may use signal words such as *because, so,* and *therefore* to show cause and effect. Draw a two-column chart on the board with the headings *Cause* and *Effect(s)*. Complete the chart after students finish the story.

Directed Reading: "Lewis and Clark"

RETEACH Use these bulleted sentences to walk students through the story.

Pages 678–681
- In 1804, Lewis and Clark set out from St. Louis to explore America's West.
- When they stopped for the winter season, they met a trader and his wife, an Indian named Sacajawea.

Pages 682–683
- Sacajawea helped the explorers find food and travel the correct river routes.
- The expedition also met up with different Native American tribes.
- The chief of the Shoshone is Sacajawea's brother.

QUESTIONS: pages 678–683
- Did Lewis and Clark explore America's South? (*no*)
- What did Sacajawea do? (*She helped the explorers find food and travel the correct river routes.*)

Pages 684–685
- Crossing the Rocky Mountains was one of the most difficult parts of the trip.
- The expedition crossed the Rocky Mountains on foot.

Pages 686–687
- The expedition made canoes to travel the rivers to reach the Pacific Ocean.
- The explorers had some problems dealing with the Chinook Indians.

Pages 688–689
- Lewis and Clark reached the Pacific Ocean in 1805.
- President Jefferson gave them a letter of credit.
- Sacajawea is remembered for helping the expedition to succeed.

Pages 690–691
- Lewis and Clark wrote in journals about their experiences.
- You can visit the historic sites along the route the explorers traveled.

QUESTIONS: pages 684–691
- Did Lewis and Clark cross the Rocky Mountains on horses? (*no*)
- What did President Jefferson give to the explorers to pay for a ship ride home? (*a letter*)

FLUENCY PRACTICE Ask a volunteer to read a paragraph from page 680 aloud. Encourage students to describe the illustrations on *Pupil Edition* 684–685 using as many vocabulary words as they can in their descriptions.

BEFORE

Making Connections
pages 694–695

Build Background: "Cross Country"

PRETEACH Remind students that "Lewis and Clark" is about men who explored the new Western territory in the United States. In "Cross Country" they will read about Terri, a girl who is going to travel across the country on vacation. Like Lewis and Clark, Terri writes about her experiences in a journal.

English-Language Learners Book

Concept Words
leave
trip
road map
campfire
sights
stars

Write the concept words on the board. Use them in sentences to illustrate their meanings.

- I **leave** tomorrow with my family to go on vacation.
- I'm excited about our **trip** to Florida.
- My parents will use a **road map** to find the right way to get to Florida.
- When we go camping, we cook food over the **campfire**.
- There are many **sights** in Florida, like the ocean, palm trees, and beaches.
- The **stars** in the sky at night look wonderful.

Have students add these words to their Language Dictionaries

AFTER

Skill Review
pages 696–697

Directed Reading: "Cross Country"

Summary *Terri isn't very excited about her family's camping vacation. However, she soon becomes more and more interested in the sights she sees.*

Use these sentences to walk students through the story.

Pages 2–3
- Their family is going on a camping trip across the United States.
- The family will sleep in a camper.
- Terri doesn't want to go on the trip.

Pages 4–7
- They are using a road map to find what roads to take.
- The family stops at a campground.

QUESTIONS: pages 2–7
- Does Terri want to go on the trip? (*no*)
- What did Terri's parents use to find what roads to take? (*a road map*)

Pages 8–11
- Terri thought maybe the trip would be okay.
- Terri saw the Black Hills of South Dakota and Mt. Rushmore.
- That night, the family went to another campground.

Pages 12–16
- The next morning they went to Yellowstone Park.
- The next day the family saw a waterfall.
- Then they saw Old Faithful which is a geyser that shoots hot water.
- Finally the family visited the Grand Canyon.

QUESTIONS: pages 8–16
- Did Terri see Mt. Rushmore? (*yes*)
- What did Terri see at Yellowstone Park? (*animals, Old Faithful*)

Focus Skill Main Cause and Effect

RETEACH Review the definitions of *cause* and *effect* with students. Then draw on the board a two-column chart with the headings *Cause* and *Effect(s)*. Ask students to revisit the story to complete the chart.

FLUENCY PRACTICE Ask students to read page 5 aloud. Then, have students use the illustrations on page 12–13 to retell part of "Cross Country" using as many vocabulary words and concept words as possible.

Independent Writing: Expedition Journal

PRETEACH Tell students that they are going to write an entry in an expedition journal about a trip that they took. Generate a concept web in the center circle with the phrase *My trip to* _____. Have students work in pairs or in small groups to brainstorm a trip to write about. Then have them brainstorm descriptive words and phrases to describe the trip.

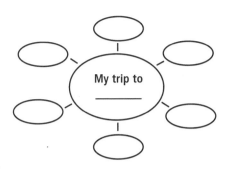

My trip to
_____

Have students write an entry in an expedition journal. Encourage them to use the concept web that they completed to describe their trip. Tell students that an expedition journal organizes experiences in chronological order. Have students reread the entry to help them plan what to write next.

Grammar: Comparing with Adverbs

PRETEACH Discuss the definition of an *adverb* that compares with students. Point out the following:

- **Adverbs** can be used to compare actions. When you compare one action with another, add *-er* to most short adverbs. Use *more* if the adverb has two or more syllables.
- When you compare one action with two or more other actions, use the superlative form that adds *-est* to most short adverbs. Use it if the adverb has two or more syllables.
- Some adverbs have special forms for comparison. For example the comparative form of *well* is *better*. The superlative form of *well* is *best*.

Write the following sentences on the board. Ask students to give the correct comparative form of the adverb in parentheses:

1. Billy couldn't wait (*long*) to leave. (*longer*)
2. Terri's mom checked the road map (*often*). (*more often*)
3. Terri didn't feel (*well*) about leaving her friends. (*better*)
4. Terri (*excitedly*) wrote in her journal. (*more excitedly*)
5. The trip seemed to be going (*fast*). (*faster*)

FLUENCY PRACTICE Have volunteers read aloud the expedition journal entry that they completed in the writing activity.

Independent Writing: Expedition Journal

RETEACH Have volunteers read their journal entries aloud. Ask the class what they might change about it and why. Discuss students' suggestions for changing to or adding to the journal entries. Have students revise their journal entries. Then have students copy their revised expedition journal entries into their Language Journal.

Remind student to check the use of adverbs that compare in their journal entries.

Grammar-Writing Connection

RETEACH Review adverbs that compare with students. Write these sentences on the board and read them aloud with students:

> *Lewis and Clark felt better during their trip when Sacajawea helped them.*

> *Terri felt better during her trip when she saw Old Faithful.*

Ask students to identify the comparative adverb in the sentence above. Then, suggest students work in pairs to draw one scene from either "Lewis and Clark," "Cross Country," or a trip of their own. Encourage students to describe their pictures aloud. Then work with them to write a sentence or two that uses adverbs that compare to describe their pictures. Check student's writing and suggest any corrections they need to make.

FLUENCY PRACTICE Have students describe their pictures out loud to the class.

Name _____

You are going to design a postcard for a trip that you took. In the first space below, draw a picture for the front of your postcard. Then in the second space, write a short letter to a friend, telling him or her about your trip.

© Harcourt

TO THE TEACHER You may want to show students some real postcards. Have students draw the design for the front of the postcard first. Then you may want to model how to write the address on the right side on the back of the card and the letter on the left. Have students read their letters aloud for sense.

LESSON 30

Use with "Black Frontiers"

BEFORE

Building
Background
and Vocabulary

Build Background/Access Prior Knowledge

Have students look at the photographs on *Pupil Edition* 709. Point to the families and tell students that they are pioneers who traveled west to find a new place to live. Ask: **How do you think traveling to a new place to live made the pioneers feel? What did the pioneers have to do to live in a new place?** Record their responses in a chart like this one:

Traveling to a new place to live made the pioneers feel	
scared	because they might not be able to grow food or crops
excited	would have a new home
nervous	would have a lot of hard work and chores

Selection Vocabulary

PRETEACH   Display Teaching Transparency 281 and read the words aloud. Then point to the pictures as you read the following sentences:

1. The man has **designated** or chose two of the men to work.
2. Many years ago in the United States people **migrated** to the west to live. They moved from one region of the country to another.
3. Here we see an **exodus**. Many people are going away from the town.
4. Some people pay in **installments** when they buy something. They pay smaller payments at regular times.
5. The man **burrowed** into the ground. He dug into the ground.

AFTER

Building
Background
and Vocabulary

Selection Vocabulary

RETEACH   Revisit Teaching Transparency 281. Read the words with students. Have students work in pairs to discuss the meanings of the words and to answer questions such as: Does **exodus** mean to *come to* or to *go away* from? Does **installments** mean *smaller parts* or *whole?*

Write the following sentence frames on the board. Read each sentence and ask students to choose a vocabulary word to complete it. Write students' responses in the blanks.

1. The dog _____ in the backyard. (*burrowed*)
2. Last winter the birds _____ from the north to the south. (*migrated*)
3. After the concert ended, there was an _____ from the auditorium. (*exodus*)
4. My teacher _____ me to write on the board. (*designated*)
5. They bought the land by paying in _____. (*installments*)

Have students write these words in their Language Dictionaries.

FLUENCY PRACTICE   Have students read the sentence frames aloud. Encourage them to describe the illustrations on Teaching Transparency 281 using the vocabulary words and any other words they know.

---

176   Lesson 30 • *English-Language Learners Teacher's Guide*

BEFORE

Reading
"Black Frontiers"
pages 700–710

Build Background: "Black Frontiers"

Revisit the pictures on *Pupil Edition* pages 709. Tell students that the families are African American settlers. Explain that African American settlers moved west after the Civil War to find land. Discuss with students how someone might feel moving to a different region of a country (scared, excited).

DISTANT
VOYAGES

 Summarize and Paraphrase

PRETEACH Tell students that when you *summarize*, you tell briefly the main idea and important details of a passage or story. When you *paraphrase*, you restate the ideas in the passage or story in your own words without changing the meaning of the original text. Draw a K-W-L chart on the board. Tell students that homesteading was hard. Write this information in the first column of the chart. Then, write the following question in the second column: **How did pioneers build houses?** Complete the K-W-L chart when students finish the story.

Reading
"Black Frontiers"

Directed Reading: "Black Frontiers"

RETEACH Use these bulleted sentences to walk students through the story.

Pages 700–705

- These are African American pioneers.
- This man is building his house of dirt, or sod.
- Here is a finished house made of sod. It is a homestead in Nebraska.
- In the southwest built houses from mud bricks.
- There weren't many black settlers at first. Some families were lonely for company.

QUESTIONS:
pages 700–705

- Were there African American pioneer families? (*yes*)
- What did pioneer families build their houses out of? (*dirt or sod*)

Pages 706–707

- This is Benjamin Singleton. He used to be a slave.
- He started a black settlers' communities in Dunlap, Kansas.
- This is a flier he made to tell people about Kansas.

Pages 708–709

- This child is standing in front of the school in his settlement community.
- The family in the top picture was named the Shores. They were musicians.
- Another family is shown outside their house.

Page 710

- The black communities grew and prospered.
- One town formed the first black baseball team.
- This is Satchel Paige, a famous black pitcher, played ball in Nicodemus.

QUESTIONS:
pages 706–710

- Were the Shore family doctors? (*no*)
- Who started the first big black communities in Kansas? (*Benjamin Singleton*)
- Who was Satchel Paige? (*He was a famous black pitcher.*)

> **FLUENCY PRACTICE** Ask a volunteer to read a paragraph from page 704 aloud. Encourage students to describe the photographs on *Pupil Edition* 702–703 using as many vocabulary words as they can in their descriptions.

BEFORE
Making
Connections
pages 712–713

Build Background: "Westward, Bound!"

PRETEACH Remind students that "Black Frontiers" is about African American settlers, people who moved west to build homes. In "Westward, Bound!" they will read more about African American settlers. Ask students what they think the settlers had to do to live in a new place.

English-
Language
Learners
Book

Write the concept words on the board. Use them in sentences to illustrate their meanings.
- I like visiting my relatives in their **homes**.
- I was **scared** that I wouldn't have friends when I moved.
- The **pioneers** were the first people to move to the west of the United States.
- We burn wood in our **fireplace** during the winter.
- The farmer planted **crops** to grow for food.
- Washing the dishes is one of the **chores** that I do at home.

Have students add these words to their Language Dictionaries

Concept Words
homes
scared
pioneers
fireplace
crops
chores

AFTER
Skill Review
pages 714–715

Directed Reading: "Westward, Bound!"

📖 **Summary** *African American families moved to the West after the Civil War. They built houses and grew crops. They built their own towns and prospered.*

Use these sentences to walk students through the story.

Pages 2–5
- After the Civil War, many African Americans wanted their own homes.
- Many African Americans decided to move to the West to live.
- These are pioneers. They were the first people who traveled west.
- The pioneers took with them all the things they would need.

Pages 6–7
- Some people built sod houses.
- If there were a lot of trees, some people built log cabins.

QUESTIONS: pages 2–7
- Did African Americans want their own land? (*yes*)
- What do we call the first people who traveled west? (*pioneers*)

Pages 8–13
- The houses had only one room.
- After the settlers built their houses, they planted crops.
- Living in a pioneer home took a lot of hard work.
- Everyone had chores to do.

Pages 14–16
- Some children went to school.
- Most of these schools had one room and one teacher.
- More and more African American pioneers traveled to the West.

QUESTIONS: pages 8–16
- How many rooms did pioneer houses have? (*one*)
- What were the schools like? (*They had one room and one teacher.*)

★ (Focus Skill) Summarize and Paraphrase

RETEACH Review *summarizing* and *paraphrasing* with students. Then draw on the board a K-W-L chart. Ask students to revisit the story and complete the chart with information from the text.

FLUENCY PRACTICE Ask students to read page 11 aloud. Have students use the illustration on pages 4–5 to retell part of "Westward, Bound!" Encourage them to use as many vocabulary words and concept words as possible.

Independent Writing: Friendly Letter

PRETEACH Tell students that they are going to write a friendly letter to a classmate about a recent event at home or at school. Generate a list of questions that will help them plan the letter:

1. What is my *topic*?
2. Who is my *audience*?
3. What are the *main ideas* and *details* that I want to include?
4. How should I *conclude* the letter?

Have students write the letter. Encourage them to reread it frequently to plan what to write next.

Grammar: Prepositional Phrases

PRETEACH Discuss the definition of a preposition with students. Point out the following:

- A preposition is a word that tells the relationship of a noun or pronoun to another word in the sentence.
- The **object of the preposition** is the noun or pronoun that follows a preposition.
- A **prepositional phrase** is made up of a preposition, the object of the preposition, and and words in between.
- Common prepositions include *for, from, in, to, with, by, of, into, on, at, over, under, before, after, during, until*.

Write the following sentences on the board. Ask students to identify the preposition in the first three sentences. Then have them complete the next two sentences with an appropriate *preposition*.

1. The settlers lived in Kansas. (*in*)
2. They brought what they needed with them. (*with*)
3. The life of a settler was hard. (*of*)
4. The pioneers traveled _____ the West. (*to*)
5. They traveled _____ wagon. (*by*)

You may want to have students go back and identify the object of the preposition in each sentence.

FLUENCY PRACTICE Have volunteers read aloud the friendly letter that they completed in the writing activity.

Independent Writing: Friendly Letter

RETEACH Have volunteers read their letters aloud. Ask them what they would change about their letters and why. Discuss students' suggestions for changing or adding to the letter. Use the following questions to help guide students in revising their letters:

- Is the topic clearly stated?
- Are the ideas listed in a logical order?
- Does the letter have a conclusion?
- Is the letter written in the friendly letter format?

Have students revise their letters. Then have students copy the revised letter into their Language Journals.

Grammar-Writing Connection

RETEACH Write these sentences on the board and read them aloud with students:

The African American pioneers lived in sod houses.

They heated their homes with fireplaces.

Ask volunteers to underline the prepositional phrases in the sentences above. Then, have students work in pairs or in a small group to discuss what their homes are like. Ask students to draw a picture to show their ideas. Encourage students to describe their pictures aloud. Then work with them to write a sentence or two using prepositions to describe their homes. Remind students that a preposition tells the relationship of a noun or pronoun to another word in the sentence. Check student's writing and suggest any corrections they need to make.

FLUENCY PRACTICE Have students share their illustrations with the class and read their descriptive sentences aloud.

Name _____

Imagine that you are one of the pioneers. Complete the list below with some of your chores. Then draw a picture of yourself doing one of the chores. Write a sentence or two to describe your drawing. Write your sentences in your Language Journal.

Chores

_____

_____

_____

_____

TO THE TEACHER Ask students: What are some chores that you would have to do if your parents were pioneers? You may want to model some chores, such as feed the animals or take care of my younger brother. Then have students draw themselves doing one of the chores. Have them read their sentences aloud for sense. Then have them copy their sentences into their Language Journals.

Black Frontiers/Westward, Bound! • **Lesson 30** **181**

© Harcourt